BATTLE TO WIN

Pressing Through Pain for a God-sized Outcome

40-Day Devotional

Journal

Armando Palazzo

Printed in the United States of America
2020 First Edition
10 9 8 7 6 5 4 3 2 1

Subject Index:
Palazzo, Armando
Title: Win in the Struggle: Pressing Through Pain For a God-sized Outcome
1. Christian Personal Growth 2. Christian Counseling 3. Christian Death & Grief
4. Christian Self-Help 5. Christian Inspiration 6. Christian Counseling and Recovery

Paperback ISBN: 978-0-578-73791-1 Library of Congress Card Catalog Number: 2020914323

www.apmedia.com

Praises for Winning the Battle...

"Stranded in a desert of grief and pain? As a pastor myself, I've seen just how much God can do in 40 days. Just as the Spirit led Jesus into the desert for fasting, prayer, and ultimate victory over Satan, Armando's comforting words throughout this devotional remind us that 'Jesus made it out of the desert, and so will you.' Armando's passionate desire to serve the Church and his community combined with his unique experience as both a pastor AND a licensed mental health counselor makes him a trustworthy guide for all those journeying with Jesus through a personal desert of loss and grief."

Tim Lucas, founder and lead pastor of Liquid Church, author of *Liquid Church: 6 Powerful Currents to Saturate Your City for Christ*

"*Battle to Win* is grounded in the Word of God, written by a man of integrity and authenticity. Armando provides a private, guided 40-day vulnerable journey to understand and process your tender grief story in a mentally, emotionally and spiritually healthy way. This is a raw, genuine, cathartic, and purposeful devotional. It is definitely a must-read!"

Dr. Steiner, Ph.D., LPC, LMHC
http://wellsprings.org/

"The days in which we live can be dark and challenging. Hope seems scarce and uncertainty seems to be constant. How does one respond to devastating and heart-breaking news? Where does one turn when receiving a painful report? As people of faith, we turn to our Savior, Jesus Christ, and sometimes we need a friend to walk alongside us through the storm as well. Through *Battle to Win: Pressing Through Pain for a God-Sized Outcome*, Armando Palazzo becomes that "come-alongside," kind of friend. With raw and deep transparency, Armando will lead you through God's powerful work in his life, because God has the same outcome in mind for you too. As you daily read *Battle to Win*, God will heal your heart, your hurt, and you'll receive one of the most powerful tools to maintain your healing and wholeness; HOPE. Armando has been a personal friend of mine for many years and I can attest to his sincerity and genuine walk with Christ. As a pastor, I highly recommend *Battle to Win* for every minister, counselor and Christian to help deal with the "stuff" of life. My only regret while reading *Battle to Win* was that it wasn't written 20 years ago. What a wonderful tool this book would have been for so many I have known. My heart is grateful for Armando sharing his heart with us in this book. I am confident you will feel the same when you are finished reading, *Battle to Win* too.

Greg Williamson, D.Min., D.D.
Lead Pastor
Valley Christian Church

"Grieving should be something that Christians do naturally because loss is a natural part of life. Sadly, it is not. There is hardly any space for Christians to grieve when a loss is sustained. Sometimes it is because we over-spiritualize our loss, or sometimes, it is because the Church creates a superficial environment where our struggles are not welcomed. Armando Palazzo's *Battle to Win* will guide Christians who are struggling to take steps where they can find the courage to grieve and find healing and strength from our heavenly Father. If you have never grieved or are struggling to grieve, please pick up this devotional, and may God bring healing into your life."

Peter Ahn
Lead Pastor of Metro Community Church

"This heart-felt devotional was birthed through tears. Through Armando's guidance we learn to pray our pain, process our pain, and worship through our pain. We learn to hope deeply and suffer well, one day at a time."

Jarrod Jones
Senior Pastor
Grace Community Church | Orange County, NY

Dedication

⸙

This book is dedicated to all of those courageous enough to face their pain, wounds, losses, and setbacks of life. This journey is hard, it can be rough at times.

However, there is nothing as sweet as meeting God in the midst of your pain. In some ways you cannot know God apart from pain. You meet Him as rescuer when you need rescuing. As Savior when you need saving. As redeemer when you need redeeming. As Hope when you are feeling hopeless. He brings life where there is death, ruin, and setbacks. He is the God who tore open the grave. He is the God of rebirth. The God of resurrections, the God of new beginnings. It is my belief that God has a new beginning waiting for you.

Acknowledgments

In writing this Devotional, *Win in the Struggle: Pressing Through Pain For a God-sized Outcome*, I want to say thank you to all of those who journeyed with my family and I through some really difficult and hard times. In the storms of life you were there. Thank you!

As I think about my parents and siblings, you guys rock! You were there for us no matter what time or need. You are an example of what a family ought to be and I am blessed by your willingness to be present and your love and support.

A special thank you Leticia Caroccio who gave her countless hours in review of this work. Your feedback and support was so needed and valued. You have provided a special contribution and you have my deepest gratitude.

I would like to thank Christopher Palumbo and Joel Santiago. You are both men of great character and integrity. You both stood with me through one of the most difficult storms of my life without wavering. You stood for me when I could not. Thank you for being such an emotional and spiritual rock.

Pastor Joe and Ruth Nieves thank you! You were there when the darkest hour was upon us. You prayed with us and were present for our family. Thank you for all you do and who you are.

I would like to thank Ted Barnett for your friendship, support, and counsel regarding this book. You provided direction when I felt lost in this process.

To my book coach Kim Rouse, thank you so much for all you do. Working with you has been such a gift and a blessing. You are so insightful and gifted. I entrusted to you in this book my heart and our story. You were supportive, encouraging, and challenging when it was needed. God has blessed you to be a blessing and I was a recipient of that blessing. Thanks again!

I would like to thank my family. To my wife and kids; you are giants in my life. I am humbled by the courage and the strength that you possess and exhibited during these trials that we faced together. To my wife Jo Marie, you are such a blessing and gift from God to me and our children. I am blessed by you and the strength God has given you. I am thankful that you are my companion in this life journey. You have stood with me, cried with me, and celebrated God's miracle with me. Thank you!

To my daughter that has been the inspiration for this book. I am so proud of you and the woman you have become. You are strong, resilient, and courageous. You inspire me. You have encouraged me in my faith and strengthened me in weakness. You are an example of what hope in God looks like. I have seen a miracle of God in your life and ours. We have journeyed through the storm together with God. Thank you for not wavering. Thank you for who you are.

Most of all, I am thankful to the Lord for His unfailing love and faithfulness. You have sheltered us in the storms of life and brought healing where there was nothing but pain. You have never left us or abandoned us no matter how difficult the journey was. You are faithful to Your Word and I will forever put my trust in You.

Philippians 4:6-7 (NIV)

[6] Do not be anxious about anything, but in every situation, by prayer and petition, with thanksgiving, present your requests to God. [7] And the peace of God, which transcends all understanding, will guard your hearts and your minds in Christ Jesus.

2 Corinthians 1:20 (NIV)

[20] For no matter how many promises God has made, they are "Yes" in Christ. And so through him the "Amen" is spoken by us to the glory of God.

Contents

Foreword

Life-altering trauma surrounds us. Trauma may be in our families. Trauma may be inside of us. We process trauma or fail to process trauma in the ways that others modeled for us. The best we know... or can learn... how. For many of us, we learn how to process trauma through the experience of trauma. In the fog of real-time... coping as we crawl toward healing.

We also try to be present with others in their trauma. Strangers. Community members. Those we most love. Being present while they are in their pain, simultaneously while we are in our pain. It is courageous work, and breathtakingly difficult. That white-hot pain, the confusion, the feeling of inadequacy and doom... all made worse when we lack guidance. The question "am I doing this right"? We need a system that can allow us to begin to cope with the wound and also invite us to help the ones we love better. I needed that system—a guide.

In my story, the pain came to my entire family, all at once, in a morning. Perhaps, in the first weeks, as the numbness left, I felt the most out of control and frightened. As I felt the waves of grief, I lacked clarity on where to start and what to do. I needed a playbook to point me toward a direction and walk through my own grief as I supported grieving children and a spouse. Parents, leaders, and pastors need a powerful set of resources to navigate trauma. When you are in the pain, you need a guide that has been there to the dark place of grief.

Battle to Win is a monumental resource, created out of the painful experience of Armando Palazzo, but now, available to you and I, useful to anyone walking through the dark places of grief. The pace of "Battle to Win" is compassionate but determined. *Battle to Win* will allow you to make progress, salted with rest and compassion. The format of *Battle to Win* is brilliant, inviting the grieving reader to experience community with the author's deep moments and then move into facilitated journaling. Perhaps the journaling is the most important part of the book. Telling your story for the first time, as you process. That was so helpful to me.

The book is hard, kind, and effective. It was the confidence that I needed to tell my story and move me along my pathway toward healing, as I encouraged those I love.

Christopher Palombo
Nonprofit Executive, trauma survivor, and Christ-follower

INTRODUCTION

You Are Not Alone

"Pain is a part of life, but it is God who brings purpose to it."

- Armando Palazzo

There were five distinct moments in my life where grief, despair, and pain was so deep, that it pierced the depths of my soul physically and emotionally. I sensed the leading of the Holy Spirit that it was time to develop my raw, uncut prayers, into a devotional book that helped deliver me from a time of great despair. It was clear that this would be a 40-day devotional to support others in their time of need.

When Jesus was led out into the desert where he fasted, prayed, and was tested for 40 days,[1] His season in the wilderness was also a time of pain. My journey of pain felt like I was in a desert, a wilderness, and left all alone. It was my time of testing, deep pain, and deep faith. I am a year and a half into my journey of discovery and my faith has strengthened. Jesus made it out of the desert and so will you.

The words grief, loss, or pain, often cause us to think that it must be the result of a death. Yet there are many kinds of deaths or losses we face in this life. Grief is experienced in a much wider range of losses than just the physical loss of a loved one. Some experience grief as a result of having lost a career, a beloved pet, financial ruin, sickness, betrayal, an unfilled dream, breakup of a relationship, unresolved family conflict, trauma, social shame, a traumatic event, a wayward child, divorce, and the list goes on and on. Grief may be the result of *any* loss of something or someone that is significant in our life to cause great emotional distress.

In addition to being a pastor, I work bi-vocationally as a licensed mental health counselor. Over the years, many clients described psychosomatic pains, which I had not known first hand until now. My clients were open to share with me that their grief or sense of loss was so bad they didn't know if they would survive. I now fully and completely understand what they meant. Others have expressed the benefit and release from journaling. I had never journaled. However, at this crossroad in my life, I had no choice.

In this devotional you will notice though I share the pain, impact and aftermath of the traumatic event in which I don't share the details of the event at length. It was a struggle to decide whether to share details of the trauma that was before us; but through much prayer and consideration for our child, I decided I would share the journey, the feelings and the struggle rather than the details of the trauma itself. This was a thoughtful boundary to protect our child from the re-trauma of exposure. If you are a parent, I am confident that you understand this sensitivity and need to protect. The details of this event are really her story to share one day when she is ready. It is her testimony and her strength. So, this devotional is the story of what we faced as a family, and how it profoundly impacted each of us.

It all started when my oldest was about 14 years of age. She began to struggle with depression, engaged in self harm, and had suicidal ideation. This was a very desperate and trying time in our lives. As parents, we lived in a state of constant fear that we would come home one day and find that our worst fears have been actualized. We could not make sense of our fear for her safety and the impact upon our other children. How could our happy loving child who has always loved life now despise it so much? What could have brought her here?

What has happened?

Nothing in life could have prepared me for this pain; not my career in counseling, my calling as a pastor, nor theology. I had no answer for it.

I couldn't fix it or make it better. All of the counseling skills and prayers didn't take my pain away. I felt utterly and completely overwhelmed and ill-equipped. My life had fallen apart and I had no response for it. I felt like a failure and distant from God. I was now left with my grief, perceived failure, and shame.

During those early moments, I was brought back to the story of Jesus in the Garden of Gethsemane. Right before his arrest, He would endure the greatest of pain and punishment. He, too, ran to the Father in prayer.[2] He felt such deep sorrow and pain to the point of death. I think we should take comfort in knowing that even Jesus, the Son of God Himself, the second member of the Trinity, knows the depth of my pain and yours.

Bringing God into our pain opens the door for how we experience this journey of pain. We *all* have to go through this journey. We can't expedite it or run through it. Nor should we try to avoid it or medicate it—that will cause more destruction and pain. In our culture we have such a fast food mentality. We live in a society where almost everything is perceived to be in our control and for our convenience. One of the few things we approach differently is working out at the gym. Very few of us expect to go to the gym for a one-time workout and expect to lose 30 pounds. Why do we not approach our faith this way?

Any fast food approach to pain leaves us with unrealistic expectations. Life is really a mixed bag of the good and the bad. Unfortunately, many of us are ill-equipped to cope and deal with difficult times. I don't know why that is, maybe the difficult things are too scary and uncomfortable. Whatever the reason, no one taught us how to suffer well.

During this deep and terrifying season, the pain I was facing was so great that all the encouragement in the world and the emotional and spiritual band aides – "pray harder," "it will get better.", "trust God," fell on deaf ears. Although at times, a part of me felt that nothing could make my situation better, the other part knew that it would only get better with God as my companion. When I think of suffering, I have to think there is more to it. When I sit in my pain, I am at a place of such great despair only God can heal. I knew ultimately that I would find peace and I would find God! I've learned that there must be purpose in pain, and it will ultimately be revealed.

The prayers in this devotional were never written with the intention of one day being a devotional book. Rather, this was birthed out of deep pain; from hitting a wall head on so hard I questioned whether myself or my family would ever recover, whether we would ever be the same. I couldn't imagine life ever being OK again.

I started writing out my prayers. It was hard to speak, to know what to say or even pray for. My emotions were all over the place and I was emotionally and spiritually confused. I was overwhelmed and had difficulty even praying, talking or expressing my feelings into words. So, I just wrote. Sometimes I wrote multiple times a day. I wrote as I needed to cry out. I viewed it more as writing out my prayers to God, than labeling it as journaling. I was writing to someone wiser and more powerful than me. I have the expectation that He hears my prayers and has the ability to respond. Knowing God was in the midst of my pain and turmoil brought me such deep hope and purpose.

"The Lord is close to the brokenhearted and saves those who are crushed in spirit."

- Psalm 34:18

I claim Psalm 34:18 over my life and the life of my family. I claim it over you and your family as well. In using this devotional, it will allow you to journey through your grief, and find hope. Each devotional has five sections:

*Prayer

*Self-Contemplation

*Scripture

* Your Daily Prayer

*Prayer Journal Questions

1. Prayer: Each devotional will start with my own personal prayer journal entries or lament from my journey.

2. Self-Contemplation: Each prayer is followed by an emotional and spiritual self-contemplation that is meant to encourage you and speak life into the confusion of your loss, grief, anger, and pain. It should help you meet God where you are in your journey.

3. Scripture: Following the self-contemplation are Scripture references that were encouraging to me and I believe will be a source of encouragement and hope to you.

4. Daily Prayer: In addition to meditating on Scriptures, confessing daily prayers in first person can help to strengthen your soul, breathe life into your situation, and help you to own your faith and the promises of God. Scripture is clear about the power of the tongue:

Proverbs 18:21 NIV

The tongue has the power of life and death, and those who love it will eat its fruit.

This power is not in the same sense of God's power to speak but rather the power of creating a self-fulfilling prophecy. What we speak will either bring life or death/negativity in a spiritual and emotional sense.

5. Prayer Journal Questions: After your daily prayer, there are questions to challenge you to process, to have the courage to feel, and to help you express your feelings to engage with God. Try to approach the questions from a conversational platform with God. Lines are provided at the end of each devotional for your own self-contemplation, questions, or prayers. If you are working through this book in a small group context, follow the same directions and then discuss the prayers/journal entries, contemplation, scriptures, and questions with your group. Share within the group your own journal entries, if you're up for the challenge.

I encourage you to use this collection of prayers more as a tool rather than just normal reading material. Generally, it is recommended that you not start writing a devotional if you are still in the shock stage of a difficult event, loss or tragedy. Emotional shock is a common response to trauma or in some cases, even vicarious trauma. Emotional shock is an acute stress reaction. Shock is usually short-term. It usually follows the first few days after a traumatic realization.

People have described being in shock in many different ways. Some people who have experienced shock have described the absence of feelings, feelings of confusion, feeling disconnected, distracted, wondering why they were not crying, or screaming. This is when you received that initial phone call or that figurative phone call—that moment your world stood still. Some of you might still be in this position today.

At this point, taking it slowly, sharing your story, allowing yourself to receive the support of those around you, and trying your best to be emotionally, physically, and spiritually present, are the best initial steps. If you have had a significant loss, you may want to consider counseling, grief care, or meet with your spiritual leaders for pastoral care and support. Don't isolate yourself. You are not alone even when it feels like it. Let someone in to support and walk with you. You matter and so do your feelings.

In addition, I have provided five rest days throughout this devotional after every eight days. One of the more important things that I found on my journey through pain and recovery in coping with the weight, the pressure, and the pain, is rest and self-care. They will bring peace to your heart and comfort to your soul. During a traumatic moment, your body, mind, soul, and spirit are working overtime. All are constantly running and racing with worry, fears, anxieties, and pain. As you know, rest and self-care look different for each of us. For me, I found the best rest and self-care was being with God in nature. Taking long hikes or fishing at a local lake or stream rejuvenated my soul. Take a breather and find something to break your routine of stress and worry. Consider doing something you've never done before, treat yourself, allow your creativity to flow, practice gratitude, limit your social media interactions, or volunteer your time.

It is my hope that this devotional will help validate you and help you find hope in the truth that there is life after a loss, failure, mistake, a setback, or even grief. One thing for certain; things will never be the same. What happened is done. There is no taking it back and there is no do over. Trust that God can use your situation as a catalyst for good and positive change in your life. Somehow, by going through this journey, you can meet God.

Read this devotional at your own pace. There is no pressure to read every day. Go back and read prayers that correlate with where you are emotionally. This journey is more about sitting in your pain long enough for it to do its work rather than trying to run out of it. There is life after loss and grief, and it can be a good life that is fun, happy, and fulfilling. Somehow, God leverages our pain for us to encounter Him and grow. Keep your eyes fixed on the prize, which is HOPE. Hope in God who knows and understands your pain. Hope in the God who will rescue you. Hope in God who is able to do more than you can imagine or think as He meets you on this journey.

As we now in courage move forward fighting through, pressing through, and pushing through the pain, there is a God-sized miracle awaiting all of us. Let's win together in the struggle. God can do more than we can ever imagine.

"The end of a matter is better than the beginning…"

- Ecc. 7:8

DAY 1

The Day the World Stood Still

"Honest questions, sincere doubts, and deep hurts can draw you closer to God than you've ever imagined before."

- Craig Groeschel

Prayer of stunned disbelief:

Lord, I do not want to accept recent tragedy. I am resistant to accepting things as they now are. I find myself avoiding it. How could this be true? How could this have happened? I don't understand.

Lord, I feel so abandoned. I feel rejected, as if your favor has been taken away. This can't be true; this can't possibly be true. Your promise is that You would never leave us nor forsake us!! I trust Your word and find myself now holding onto it desperately. I sink my nails deep inside of it to hold on, but I feel them slipping. It's so hard, I feel like I can't comprehend or process what was shared then or what's happening now. I am feeling oddly detached and numb. As I sit here in confusion, I question even if it's all real. It must not be!! How can it be??

I have so many questions. I don't know how or what to ask or if I'm even sure if I want the answers. I just want to go to sleep and wake up from this bad nightmare. I want to find out that this was all a terrible dream. It's not real, it's not happening. Please give me the strength to face this. I am so fearful. I'm terrified. I have never felt terror before.

1

As I look for meaning, I search Your Scriptures. I find story after story of the heroes of old; the stories of men and women of God who walked through disastrous situations to eventually find them where You were faithful in seeing them through their journey and faithful to Your promise in the end.

I know I am struggling with shock and denial of the current situation. I don't want it. How can I possibly want it? Yet I know that you have a purpose in it and in the end will make it good because I love you and I know you love me.

At this moment, I cannot make sense of it, though. I can only hope that at some point clarity would be revealed to me. You're faithful to turn a bad situation into good and to turn the waste into a harvest. I'm just broken, beaten, and exhausted. I'm so tired and overwhelmed. All I have the energy for is to still hope; to just sit and hope this wasn't real. Please do for my family and me what I am powerless to do!

Emotional & Spiritual Self-Contemplation:

Have you ever cried out to God in a similar manner? When nothing made sense anymore and I couldn't understand why everything was happening, I held onto one stabilizing truth: That God was real and that God was good. I just didn't understand why we were now facing what we were facing.

I knew one thing for sure: That there would be no quick fix, no matter how much I wanted one. So apart from an immediate miracle, I knew I was on a journey that would take time for myself and my family to heal. The fear and pain was just so debilitating and heavy. It hurt to breathe. There was nowhere else to go and no one else to run. All I had was God. This was a journey of wrestling.

It was a typical Tuesday morning when I received a call at work. When I answered, little did I know that the call would change everything. A family member shared devastating news. I was in complete and utter shock. Each time I asked to repeat what was said, I could not comprehend or process what I was hearing. Of course, I heard it but it was like my brain couldn't understand, compute or accept it. It was as if my brain was rejecting this news, much like a gag reflex—everything was in slow motion. It literally felt as though the world stood still.

I had so many questions that I wanted to ask but I could not articulate. All I kept saying was: "What? What? I don't understand."This must've been very confusing for the one sharing with me their devastating news, but at that moment, I just could not function. My brain wasn't working. I knew what I heard, I just couldn't understand it. I wondered what it all meant. What did this mean for our lives as a family? What did it mean for the way things were?

I wondered how Mary, Jesus' mother and the Apostles felt as Jesus would share with them prophetically His death to come?[3] They, too, received the figurative call. Jesus was sharing something with them that they could not understand; they could not make sense of. All they knew was that they did not want it. They did not want that phone call and neither did I. You didn't want your world to stand still either. None of us would choose a tragic outcome.

Three days after the phone call, I literally could not function. If you have received a phone call or can remember the exact point where your pain started, you know what I'm talking about. I did not know what to do with everything I was feeling; the confusion, the sadness, the numbness, the emotional detachment, the feeling like a zombie, emotionally and spiritually. All of these confusing feelings that I was experiencing overwhelmed me.

I had no action plan. No steps. All of my work as a counselor, all of the skills that I have used to help others navigate through grief, totally abandoned me in this painful moment. For the first time in my life I picked up a pen and cried out the best way that I could. Somehow, on paper, everything I felt started to make sense. I was able to articulate questions, share with God my desperation. Writing out my prayers seemed to be the only thing that made sense. It just kind of all happened. Looking back, it all makes sense. When faced with the greatest hardship of my life, I had nowhere to turn but back to God. I had no one else to run.

Scriptures

The following verses brought me comfort as they reminded me that God was still present in my life. Though things were now chaotic, the realization of God being with me brought me hope, though I still had so much pain. Of course, none of what happened in your situation makes sense at this early point in your journey. As you write below try to find a Scripture or promise of God to hold in your heart and mind; it's the only rock you have to stand on.

Psalm 34:18 ESV

The Lord is near to the brokenhearted
   and saves the crushed in spirit.

Deuteronomy 31:6 ESV

Be strong and courageous. Do not fear or be in dread of them, for it is the Lord your God who goes with you. He will not leave you or forsake you."

Daily Prayer

Dear Lord, in these difficult moments I pray that I will sense you now more than ever. In and of myself I lack strength and courage. I thank you that you will meet me where I am at. You comfort the brokenhearted and save those that feel lost. I pray that you would bless this journey for me and bring me hope. I turn to you now in my hurt and pain and I ask that you bless me in the name of Jesus. Amen

Prayer Journal Questions

Personal Reflections...
1. What was your experience of that initial "phone call" or moment your world stood still? Try to focus on your feelings rather than what you thought. Start with, *"I feel...."*

2. Where was God at this moment? Did you feel God was distant or close?

3. Which Scripture or promise of God are you standing on today?

DAY 2

Heart of Heaviness

"There's only one power in the world great enough to help us rise above the difficult things we face: the power of God."

- Stormie Omartian

An inconsolable hurt:

Lord, my heart feels so heavy, a weight that I am not sure I can bear. I feel burdened and afflicted with pain. As the burden gets heavier, I start to feel so numb. I can't feel anymore. This numbness is not a comforting feeling, but rather, a feeling of emptiness. There is no joy or solace in feeling numb. It causes me to be concerned for myself. I want to feel again, but I know if I open that door to the feelings, and as the numbness departs, the emptiness invites pain and sadness. I do not desire to dwell in either of these places. I am scared to death to face and accept the pain and trauma my child now faces, the weight of pain on my family, and the guilt I hold as a father.

So I cry out. I cry out for You to rescue me. I cry out because I feel like I can no longer run. I feel like I can no longer defend. I feel like I can no longer protect. I cry out because I am in need.

What does Your Word have for me? What encouragement and hope can I find there? What is Your promise to me? You are the God that rescues. You are my strong fortress. You are my rock. You bring me peace. It is Your hand that *has demonstrated faithfulness, love, and tenderness. It is Your hand that rescues and makes a way. It is by Your hand that we will be delivered.*

I feel so helpless and so empty. I just wish that I could make this all better or go away and I can't. You give hope to those who need hope, You give help to those in need of help, and You give peace to the brokenhearted. I call upon Your name, Lord, and I ask for Your blessing, Jehovah, my Provider, Jehovah, my Rescuer.

Emotional and Spiritual Self-Contemplation

As I reread this prayer of desperation, it brought me back to that deep sinking feeling of loss, of emptiness, and helplessness. I felt as if I were trying to swim while tied to a heavy weight. I was sinking fast. As I started to write this prayer, I realized that I had not yet cried. I was still in shock. My feelings seemed to have vanished. I knew tears were appropriate, but I was so shut down. A short while after I expressed this numb detached feeling in this short prayer, it happened. The dam broke loose and the tears started to flow. My tears became an uncontrollable river.

Crying out was all I could do. I cried and cried. I had no tears left. I was stunned to find that tears could run out. It was a scary feeling. I was still in shock. Not comprehending all that was happening. At this point, it still felt like a dream.

As I reflect upon this, I wondered what Jesus' followers and family felt after His body was laid in the tomb.[4] I imagine they were in an emotional state of shock. How confusing is that? Their Lord, their Savior had died. None of this made any sense. I imagine they too felt as I did and how you may now feel. What was it like to go home after Jesus was removed from the cross and laid in a tomb? It must have been terrifying, shocking, and painful. What did it all mean? Like me, I imagine they felt numb and confused. I believe the Apostles, like us, had hoped that they would wake up from this bad dream. Fortunately, their shock soon turned to joy. They woke up to the resurrection of a conquering Savior. Scripture promises us that the same power that raised Jesus from the dead is alive in us. We, too, will wake up from the shock. The following scriptures brought me connection back to reality and my emotions.

Scriptures

Roman 8:28 NIV

And we know that in all things God works for the good of those who love him, who have been called according to his purpose.

Psalm 107:13-16 ESV

"Then they cried to the Lord in their trouble, and he delivered them from their distress. He brought them out of darkness and the shadow of death, and burst their bonds apart. Let them thank the Lord for his steadfast love, for his wondrous works to the children of man! ..."

Daily Prayer

Lord, I claim your blessings over each of our journeys. I claim them in the name of Christ Jesus. What you have done and said, the enemy cannot steal or have. Thank you for the reminder of what you have done in the past because it causes me to look forward to what you will do again. It is your promises that I embrace. To God be the glory. Amen.

Prayer Journal Questions

Personal Reflections...
1. How do you connect your feelings to the experiences of Jesus' family and companions upon His death or to others that you know are hurting?

2. Describe the helplessness you feel at this point in your journey?

3. What specific help do you ask of the Holy Spirit?

DAY 3

❦

No Relief in Sight

*"My family was falling apart and I felt the weight of the
world on my shoulders.
How could I save them? What could I do to make this better?"*

- Armando Palazzo

A desperate disbelief:

*L*ord, *I wish it was all just a dream. I wish this was something I could wake
up from and life would be normal. It feels like it is always there; hovering and
contaminating every thought, experience, and moment. The anger and hurt plagues
me like a cloud that I cannot run from nor hide. At times, it feels like the anger and
rage overwhelms me and I just want to explode. I long for Your peace. I remember
what that peace once felt like. I choose to believe in the hope to come. I trust in the
healing. I know that is Your desire and plan for me and all of us. It will happen, it
must happen. Yet the waiting is so difficult. I'm not sure how long I can wait and
hold on to Your promises. It amazes me the longevity of pain that persists from just
one horrible moment. It stays with me and causes pain to me and those around me.
Thank you for those brief moments when I have gotten away from it and life feels
somewhat normal. However, the peace quickly vanishes and the pain returns when
I am alone. I prayed to You to rescue us. I asked if You would shorten the duration
of this pain. I know healing from grief is a process and often takes time. I'm just
not sure how much longer I can wait! It's too heavy and it's too painful. If it is time*

that it is going to take, please send us many more moments of peace during the in-between—not just fleeting moments. We will continue to wait on You. We will continue to trust in You and Your promises. Your Word, Your will, and Your way are all that we have to stand on. You are our Deliverer.

Emotional and Spiritual Self-Contemplation

I remember the inescapability of the pain and the obsessive thoughts that were so common. I could not bear it for another moment. I was drowning in it. During the early days of my journey, sleep was scarce. On those nights where I got a little sleep, I was still plagued with thoughts of details of what happened and what I was doing during those terrible moments for my daughter. I tried every healthy coping mechanism I could think of: prayer, reading, utilizing supports, and counseling. Even if I completed all of these tasks on the same day, they were only a short-term distraction. I could not find sustained peace.

Then the Holy Spirit spoke to me clearly. It was my light bulb moment. God told me to begin journaling. I purchased my first journal and began to write. Instantly, I felt a supernatural release. I was eager to commit to this habit as I was beginning to feel calm and have a little more control over my emotions. Prayer journaling was the only way I could face this traumatic family experience in a healthy way. Each day the release felt better. All I could do was cry for help, pray, and wait for my breakthrough.

I could not help but think of the many ways and times God had delivered the Israelite people from their oppression. The most celebrated deliverance of all is found in the Exodus of Egypt. Exodus is so important that a book bears its name. As I think over the deliverance of the Israelites, I am reminded that it was necessitated by their captivity under the Egyptians, who had enslaved them for 400 years. I wonder what it must have been like to suffer in slavery for 400 years and what impact that had on their minds. The trauma. The emotional inescapability. The frustration. More importantly, the anger.

I also felt like my mind and emotions were enslaved. It was like I had no control over my mind nor emotions. I was battered by my thoughts and confused feelings. I was suffering intrusive and obsessive thoughts of fears, anxieties, and constant worry. A challenge for me was that my worry was founded on factual grounds. My daughter struggled with depression and all of the negative thoughts and emotions that come with the trauma she experienced. My wife was slipping into a depression. My family was falling apart and I felt the weight of the world on my shoulders. How could I save them? What could I do to make this better? I was frustrated with myself because I knew I wasn't strong enough or capable enough. I need a Redeemer. I needed God more than ever before.

I found hope in the Exodus story because of the reason it was recorded in the first place—a faithful God who delivers, who remembers, who comes to our aid. Maybe the rescue was not as soon as the Israelites hoped for, or as quick as I had wanted, but I trust a God who can. Although I was in slavery to my pain and painful thoughts, Exodus gave me hope of my impending exodus and the freedom from my emotional oppression.

Scriptures

Acts 2:21 ESV
And it shall come to pass that everyone who calls upon the name of the Lord shall be saved.'

Psalm 34:17 ESV
When the righteous cry for help, the Lord hears and delivers them out of all their troubles.

Psalm 50:15 ESV
And call upon me in the day of trouble; I will deliver you, and you shall glorify me."

Daily Prayer

I take refuge in Your promise to deliver. I accept that this is reality and my pain is going through a process of recovery. As I wait, I cry out to Your name in my time of trouble. I cry for help and receive Your promise of salvation and deliverance. I claim Your deliverance over my life. Amen.

Prayer Journal Questions

Personal Reflections...
1. Have you felt a sense of inescapability of pain or thoughts?

2. What coping mechanisms are healthy and helpful to you?

3. Share with God what is happening right now in your thought life and emotions?

4. Share with Him what thoughts and emotions you are struggling with and what you need deliverance from?

5. What hope do you stand on today?

DAY 4

⌖

Sleepless Nights

"God actually delights in exalting our inability. He intentionally puts his people in situations where they come face to face with their need for him."

- David Platt

Praying through the dark night:

Lord, I struggle so much at times just to go to sleep. There are some nights that I hit the bed like a ton of bricks, emotionally, physically, and spiritually exhausted. Without even realizing it, I am in a deep slumber, off in the fantasy of a dream. But last night was tough. Not only emotionally tough, but also frustrating. Lately, sleep seems to be the only place I find peace for my thoughts, an escape. For some reason, lately it feels like sleep has been taken away from me. I feel so stripped, so broken, and so alone.

I wanted to sleep last night, but as I lay there, my thoughts started to race, like a radio with all the stations on at once. Lord, as my mind began to finally calm and my thoughts stilled, my heart and my mind began to find peace. Then, instantly I felt a jolt of worry, and my body was ready to jump out of bed. I am not sure what it was, but I immediately sensed impending doom. It was a familiar anxiety that keeps me on my toes; in a state of hyper-awareness. This led me into prayer. Though I would rather have slept through these moments of struggling and wrestling, somehow I find peace in running to Your Holy name.

Somehow those sleepless moments push me towards You and I find peace, even if it's only for that moment. It is a reprieve from being assaulted by my own mind. Will I ever be able to shake thoughts of my responsibility for others? Will I overcome my feelings of powerlessness, fear, guilt, and shame? I am thankful because somewhere in the prayer, I fell asleep. I am not sure where or when it was, all I know is that I found peace running to Your name and the next thing I remember was waking up this morning refreshed.

I am thankful that You are a God who is concerned about my humanity, and my human state of frailty. It brings me joy to know You are concerned for my struggles and You address them. I am thankful that I always have You to run to.

Emotional and Spiritual Self-Contemplation

There were many sleepless nights for quite a while during this part of my grief journey. At this point, I often approached bedtime with anxiety. I began to fear this part of my day because I knew how difficult the nights had become. It was challenging because if I could just sleep I would have the emotional break I needed and wanted; but sleep was often fleeting. I was so frustrated!

I am reminded of the Psalmist David, as he too desired rest for his weary soul.[5] David was fleeing from his enemies, who in this case just happened to be his son, Absalom. David was exhausted. He felt abandoned, rejected, and was slandered. He had deep cries of pain. He was assaulted on all sides. All that sustained him in his grief and many losses is what I too have discovered: running to the name of the Lord in the midst of my deepest agony, which happened to be nearly every evening. Those nighttime hours were always the toughest. It felt so lonely and long, assaulted by thoughts, bargaining and replaying events over and over. But the difficulties of these evenings often pushed me toward God. In my prayers of exhaustion, I found peace and rest for my weary soul.

What I was experiencing was deep grief and vicarious trauma. If you can identify with these feelings and nighttime experiences, find someone to talk to. The best thing to do with these types of emotions and exposure is to tell your story and process your pain. Maybe a counselor, a grief or trauma group, pastoral care, or even a friend can help relieve the anxiety of dealing with this on your own.

Scriptures

Psalm 3 - NIV

Lord, how many are my foes!
  How many rise up against me!
Many are saying of me,
  "God will not deliver him."
But you, Lord, are a shield around me,
  my glory, the One who lifts my head high.
I call out to the Lord,
  and he answers me from his holy mountain.
I lie down and sleep;
  I wake again, because the Lord sustains me.
I will not fear though tens of thousands
  Assail me on every side.
Arise, Lord!
  Deliver me, my God!
Strike all my enemies on the jaw;
  break the teeth of the wicked.
From the Lord comes deliverance.
  May your blessing be on your people.

Matthew 11:28-30 ESV

Come to me, all who labor and are heavy laden, and I will give you rest. Take my yoke upon you, and learn from me, for I am gentle and lowly in heart, and you will find rest for your souls. For my yoke is easy, and my burden is light.

Daily Prayer

Dear God, this journey, this pain, these trials have led me to my knees. You have brought me to a place of pain and brokenness, but I know you will not leave me here. You will strengthen me and uphold me. God you will not waste my pain as it is the fuel that builds, that strengthens, that draws me to you. This pain is the place where faith is built. Where trust is tested. My faith will persevere. God I place my trust and hope in Your work of salvation and healing. I have faced the truth that I need you more than I could ever imagine. Amen

Prayer Journal Questions

Personal Reflections...
1. Share with God how your experience has impacted your sleep and mind.

2. Discuss with God the ways you can be pushed toward God at this point in your journey. What gets in the way?

3. How can you identify with David in Psalm 3?

4. If sleep has been an issue for you, as well, what helps you to cope and what changes can you make that may help?

DAY 5

Thought Battles

*"Sometimes when you're in a dark place you think
you've been buried, but you've actually been planted."*

- Christine Caine

Praying through plaguing thoughts:

Lord, I ask, I pray, for the rest of my mind. As I go through my day, there are moments that I find myself in a tunnel of thoughts. It is like I get stuck and all I see and hear are the thoughts of those moments of pain. In those moments, I feel intense panic, anxiety, anger and rage. I feel my anger growing. It is difficult to break out of this tunnel of thoughts. Sometimes I don't even realize I am there until I am so deep in it. These are the moments where I relive the pain and it takes me captive. I try to think of other things but to no avail. What has helped is the recalling of Your name in my mind over and over and over, "Jesus, Jesus, Jesus." As I think of Your name it drowns out other thoughts. The tunnel starts to widen and I can see again. I call upon Your name in those moments and I am free. It is tiring. I am in and out of this tunnel many times a day. Yes, calling upon Your name and meditating has been freeing and helpful, even though my body and my heart are so exhausted. I am exhausted. I can't continue to fight. I feel my will giving out.

Rescue me from the tunnel of pain. I just want peace. I cannot help my thoughts. They just come upon me. They do not respect time, nor place, nor *impact. They hurt. Maybe it's my mind's way of processing all that has happened or maybe more sinister forces are at work.*

I come against you, devil, and any unhealthy thought with all the authority of my Father in Heaven. I cancel you and any strongholds in the name of Jesus. I claim back any strongholds you may have taken and any ground you have taken. I command you right now in the name of Jesus to go to the foot of my Father and go to where He shall send you. I command you to pay back with interest any bit of ground you may have stolen from my family and me. I claim freedom as a child of God. I claim victory in mind, body, soul and spirit. I claim all this in the name of my Lord Jesus Christ by the power of the Holy Spirit. Amen.

Emotional and Spiritual Self-Contemplation

I recognized that I was under assault emotionally, spiritually, and physically. Much of what I was feeling and what you are feeling today is totally normal. It's a normal part of grief and loss. However, where we are weak, the enemy, the devil, wants to exploit our weakness through negative thinking, and lies. Much like the enemy did with Jesus when He spent 40 days in the desert.

But not today! I stand with you in faith and claim a hedge of protection around you right now in the name of Jesus. There are healthy ways of coping and there are unhealthy ways, as well. At this point, I often struggled with the temptation to give myself completely over to the pain and negative thinking. For some, this might be the point where you call in your support systems, pray, engage positive self-care, or maybe for some, even seek counseling services and pastoral care.

As I contemplate over this prayer, I am reminded of God's hand of rescue. I am reminded that He is our Deliverer. I am reminded of the power of prayer. Our prayers have real power because we are communicating to a real God who cares and is concerned for us. I remember the Apostle Paul and his imprisonment, as recorded in his letter to the church in Philippi,[6] where it was only by God's hand that Paul would find peace while being imprisoned. It was only by God's hand that the Gospel could advance through Paul's chains. At this point, I remember praying for purpose in my pain. God is faithful and God doesn't waste our pain.

You may not see it now, but God will restore you and leverage your pain for good. We don't suffer like those without faith in Christ. All things will work together for good for those that love God and no weapons or attack against you will prosper. [7]

Scriptures

Psalm 34:17-20 ESV
When the righteous cry for help, the Lord hears and delivers them out of all their troubles. The Lord is near to the brokenhearted and saves the crushed in spirit. Many are the afflictions of the righteous, but the Lord delivers him out of them all. He keeps all his bones; not one of them is broken

Philippians 4:6-7 ESV
Do not be anxious about anything, but in everything by prayer and supplication with thanksgiving let your requests be made known to God. And the peace of God, which surpasses all understanding, will guard your hearts and your minds in Christ Jesus.

Psalm 107:6 ESV
Then they cried to the Lord in their trouble, and he delivered them from their distress.

Daily Prayer

Dear God, this journey can be long and difficult and rest is so desperately needed for my mind, my spirit and my body. Help me to take refuge in You and claim Your promises of restoration. I choose to stand on Your perfect record of faithfulness. Amen

Prayer Journal Questions

Personal Reflections...
1. Discuss in your prayer what you're wrestling with in your mind.
2. How do you combat the attack of the enemy on your mind, (lies, negative thinking, etc.), exploiting your natural and normal pain?

3. What self-care decisions (exercising, utilizing support systems, journal, prayer, counseling, self-help books, etc.), do you have to make?

4. What ways or strategies have been helpful in resting your mind?

5. What promises are you standing on today?

DAY 6

I Got This

"Most of us overestimate how much control we have and underestimate how much choice we have. The truth is, you never really have control, but you always have a choice. Make the choice today to stay submitted and give your control to God. He can handle things much better than you can."

- Steven Furtick

Discovering the deception of control:

Lord, I have been deceived all these years. I have deceived myself to think that I can fix everything, make everything OK, and make things better. But I cannot. This journey has taught me a lot and I am accepting my limitations, my humanity, and my brokenness. This lesson is costly. This is a very difficult truth to learn. I once thought that not having control would feel scary, overwhelming, and uncomfortable. I now realize that it is more comforting to give up control and trust the God of the universe, the God who truly has control. It's ironic. Who would have thought that accepting no control would cause me to feel safer than when I thought I had control. Through this process, I have learned much about myself, about my family, about pain, and about trusting in God. These lessons that I have learned are so valuable. I wish I could've learned it all another way under less painful *circumstances. But, this is the lot we have been given and we are learning to accept it.*

I tried fighting it, but it didn't work. I tried controlling my feelings. I tried not to feel. I'm letting go of perceived control and respecting my emotions enough to allow myself to have them and learn to sit with them. I am respecting this process and allowing the journey to go where it will. Fighting it is an illusion. I am coming to understand more deeply, to see God as a refuge, a place of safety, shelter, a rock, and a Giver of peace. Abiding in Christ through this process provides direction and safety that I would not otherwise have. God, You help me make sense of these things, even with my limited human mind. I eagerly expect in hope for full and complete restoration. Although I don't see it now, I am expecting it. That is faith. You have control. You can do for my family what I am incapable of doing. I trust You and depend on You for all things.

As a student in this situation, I know there's still much to learn. I submit my heart and mind to You, God. I desire that we would learn what You intend for us to learn during these difficult circumstances.

Emotional and Spiritual Self-Contemplation

The realization of my deception of control was revolutionary. I always knew I couldn't possibly control everything, but I went through life as if I could. I thought I could keep everyone safe. What an illusion I conjured up in my own mind due to fears of the unknown, loss, or change. Who did I think I was? I'm certainly not God! This journey has reminded me of my human frailties. The irony is that I somehow felt a comfort in finally relinquishing control or letting go of what I imagined I possessed. The comfort, I guess, was in no longer fighting and expending so much emotional, physical, and spiritual energy on a race that I could never win. There was a strange comfort and peace in the surrender.

It was really encouraging to me to remember Jesus' experience in the Garden of Gethsemane.[8] It reminded me that He was human, too, and that what I felt was OK and a normal expression of pain. Jesus, though also fully divine in His humanity, endured such deep sorrow. He felt distressed and troubled emotionally. He said, "My soul is overwhelmed with sorrow to the point of death." He quite literally felt so much emotional pain that he didn't know (figuratively speaking, of course he knew), if He would survive the pain. His pain was deep and agonizing. I was not alone. I am hoping in a God who knows exactly what I feel and He knows what you feel right now. This gives us the hope of His compassion. Jesus exemplifying this also shows me that allowing myself to feel the full range of my emotions is OK. It is culture that tells us not to feel. Culture gives us "emotional Band-Aids" such as, "You have to pray harder," "Your faith is weak," "Have joy, not sorrow," "Don't give into it," "Fight, be strong, don't let them see you cry," and similar types of admonishments hold us back from growing in our faith.

Pain, as I have always seen it, was something to run from, to hide from, and to resist. In my upbringing, I was never given the tools or the understanding of how to journey through pain. I never understood it as something God could leverage or use for good in my life. I wasn't equipped to see it as anything more than judgment, punishment, or abandonment. My family and even my past church cultures reinforced this unhealthy emotional and spiritual approach to pain. It was unbiblical.

This is a burden people and culture put on you, not God. Jesus even brought His accountability and support team with Him. He invited Peter, James, and John. He shared His tears and emotions with them. God welcomes your pain because He knows it and empathizes with you in whatever you are going through.

Scriptures

Mark 14:32-34 NIV

They went to a place called Gethsemane, and Jesus said to his disciples, "Sit here while I pray." He took Peter, James and John along with him, and he began to be deeply distressed and troubled. "My soul is overwhelmed with sorrow to the point of death," he said to them. "Stay here and keep watch."

Romans 5:3-5 ESV

Not only that, but we rejoice in our sufferings, knowing that suffering produces endurance, and endurance produces character, and character produces hope, and hope does not put us to shame, because God's love has been poured into our hearts through the Holy Spirit who has been given to us.

1 Peter 5:10 ESV

And after you have suffered a little while, the God of all grace, who has called you to his eternal glory in Christ, will himself restore, confirm, strengthen, and establish you.

Hebrews 5:7 ESV

In the days of his flesh, Jesus[a] offered up prayers and supplications, with loud cries and tears, to him who was able to save him from death, and he was heard because of his reverence.

Daily Prayer

God, I claim these promises over my life and over my family. I submit, I surrender to You in my time of need and trust that You will redeem, renew, and sanctify. To God be the glory, Amen.

Prayer Journal Questions

Personal Reflections...
1. How has the realization of your humanity and lack of control impacted your hope in God?
2. How are you able to identify with Jesus in His pain?

3. What lies has your family culture and church culture taught you about being honest and sharing your emotions?

4. How have you been changed by Jesus' model of showing emotion (something different)?

DAY 7

—⁓⁓—

How Much Longer?

"The reality is, my prayers don't change God. But, I am convinced prayer changes me. Praying boldly boots me out of that stale place of religious habit into authentic connection with God Himself."

- Lysa TerKeurst

Praying: God can we move this faster?

Lord, today is full of ups and downs. My feelings have been all over the place. I'm trying to regroup. I find it so difficult to capture in words how I feel. Again, my mind feels like a radio with all the stations playing at once. Those stations represent my emotions. It becomes increasingly difficult for me when I see others that I love hurting, mourning, and grieving like I am. I am triggered when I see others suffering and it's difficult not to commiserate. We often spiral together. It is so exhausting. I just want this nightmare to be over. I wish healing would move faster. I am so impatient right now.

I feel as powerless to help them as I can help myself. It is a humbling feeling. Thus far in my life I have known both happiness and pain. At various seasons I have experienced both and vacillated between the two. I have had the honor to walk with others through their darkest hours as well.

What I am sure of is this: that no matter what my circumstances may be, Your promises are all I can depend on. I take refuge in my Savior and hope in Your promise to use these challenging times for my good.

What purpose is faith if I don't trust You? God I know you can turn a situation around! What value is faith if we can't expect God to show up and to heal? Walking away from You isn't an option. Where else would I go? What other hope is there? None! There is no refuge but in the arms of Christ, my Lord. I find peace in You!

Only You can do for my family what I cannot. I am incapable. It has only been by Your strength, hope in Your Word, and the healing by faith that has held me above water. I may be broken, but I am not crushed. Life may feel like a train wreck, but we are not defeated. You are our Rock and our Refuge. We have spent many days fighting the never-ending stream of thoughts, memories, and anxieties. I desire rest for my family and rest for my soul. We pray that we will find favor with You. Please, please expedite our healing.

Emotional and Spiritual Self-Contemplation

Sometimes when you have nothing left all you can do is look back and remember what God has done. I choose to remember the miracles, the parting of the Red Sea, the many that were delivered by His hand, and I take comfort in knowing that you and I will have similar testimonies of deliverance. I had to look back at God's resume because it reminded me of hope and the rescue to come.

What I love most about prayer is its power and longevity. Prayers have a transcendent value. There are some prayers in life that will not be answered immediately, but there are others that will be answered throughout our lives or into the generations that follow. I am a third-generation Christ follower. I know Christ today because of prayers my grandparents prayed over me long before I was born. They prayed for the future of their family. They prayed for unhealthy family patterns to be broken and Christ to be the foundation of our new family. Claiming something in prayer has an eternal value because we are praying to an eternal God who is outside of time and space. Time is irrelevant in the Heavenly realms. God answers *all* of your prayers that are prayed within His will.

Praying constantly, over and over, sometimes for the same thing are some of the most powerful prayers. Praying and making your prayers and petitions known to God sometimes may feel monotonous and you may even feel like it's pointless or useless, but remember the time you put into prayer is the price you will pay for the miracle that will follow. I am reminded at this moment of Habakkuk's cries in plea of desperation before God. He felt like God was not answering or maybe God wasn't present. Many of us can get that feeling prayer after prayer, day after day, week after week seeking the face of God and your answer has not come yet. I find hope in the Lord's reply to Habakkuk. The Lord replies, "Look at the nations and watch— and be utterly amazed. For I am going to do something in your days that you would not believe, even if you were told." Keep praying and keep pressing forward. And be utterly amazed for God is going to do something you can't even imagine.

What are you praying and seeking God for today? Are you praying for your recovery after the loss of a loved one? Is it that cancer diagnosis? Is it that sickness? Is it financial ruin? Is it a broken relationship? Is it a loss of your career? Did your house burn down? Have you lost everything? Don't give up praying. It's your lifeline. You have to keep praying and praying hard, don't stop—don't ever stop!

Scriptures

Psalm 40:13 NIV
Be pleased, O Lord, to deliver me! O Lord, make haste to help me!

Numbers 6:24-26 NIV

The LORD bless you and keep you;
the LORD make his face to shine upon you and be gracious to you;
the LORD lift up his countenance upon you and give you peace.

Daily Prayer

Lord, I look up to the heavens and see where my help comes from. I thank you that I can look forward to a new day. With you God, there are new beginnings, rebirths, fresh starts, and do-overs. Seasons in life can feel long at times, but You are my Way Maker. Strengthen me to endure the journey.

Prayer Journal Questions

Personal Reflections...
1. What has it been like for you to experience the ups and downs of emotions?
2. How have been you impacted by the emotions and pain of others?

3. What is it you need from God today?

4. What prayers are you unwilling to give up on? Share with God the struggle of prayers that feel unheard.

DAY OF REST

As we look forward to a day of rest together let's stop and acknowledge that it has been a long week that we are carrying more than we would like. It's going to take courage for us to rest. When we are dealing with losses of relationships, loved ones, the loss of a job, or the devastation of a house fire, it is common for us to feel like we have to manage the crisis, hold the world together, and fix everything. Of course, we now know this is not possible. Remember Jesus' statement; Therefore do not worry about tomorrow, for tomorrow will worry about itself. Each day has enough trouble of its own.[9] What I am sure of is that what we have is today. Let's make today count. Let's live today with no regrets and seize the day as the day of much-needed rest and reprieve.

The power of meditating in prayer is profound. I was working once with a gentleman that seemed to have it all, at least on the outside. He had a seven-figure job, multimillion dollar home, and every imaginable comfort money can buy. Yet he was miserable. He worked so much he would often stop and think to himself how sad it was that every time he saw his children, he felt like they grew. Now, you know that's a problem, when you can tell someone is growing.

When you have not seen someone in a while or as in this case you have been so emotionally and physically unavailable, you can see changes easily. He and I started to work together to grab hold of his life and make necessary changes. He came in grieving at the loss of the life he wanted for the life of stress, anxiety, and lack of fulfillment that he created.

He started with meditation and prayer. This seemed to place things right into perspective for him. He realized the disconnect between his value system and his behaviors. It wasn't long before he started to make changes. For the first time, he started to hear the voice of God and sense His leading again.

* Limit your distractions. What competes for your time and attention?

* Set aside social media and anything that you may have identified as a source of distraction and focus on self-care. Recent studies have shown us that with increasing social media use leads to increasing depression and anxiety. Social media has also been linked to increased feelings of loneliness, weight gain, and lack of attention. Social media is bad self-care.

* Select a Scripture or a verse that has brought you hope in this journey, pick a truth or a promise from God that you can stand on. Take it with you to a relaxing room or an environment of your choosing that feels sacred, safe, and comfortable. Set your clock on two minutes or more if you can and recite that prayer, that Scripture, that truth to yourself slowly over and over. As you speak it,-feel it's comfort, feel it's promise, and hold onto its truth.

Perform the same meditation exercise many times throughout your day of rest.

✱ Pick up the phone and call a friend. Maybe, invite a friend over. Let's put down the counterfeit texting and engage in real relationships.

End the day with rest, prayer, and meditation.

DAY 8

———— ⚜ ————

Seeing Through the Pain

"Anger is the result of love. It is energy for defense of
something you love when it is threatened."

- Timothy Keller

A burning fire within me:

Lord, it angers me to see my loved ones in pain. It is a righteous anger. It is so frustrating that I have no place to direct my anger. I know You fight on our behalf. I trust You. Sometimes the rage within me just brings me to a breaking point of just spilling over. The impact of loss and grief is so profound. The aftermath feels so unjust. One single event is bad enough, but it continues to steal and compound the trauma. My entire family is in such pain. I realize that my anger originates from somewhere deep within and is made worse by my own past wounds. The anger is sharp and deep, like a sword that slices. I am much more sensitive now to the pain of others. It leaves me with a heightened sense of need for perceived justice.

I struggle with wanting control, wanting revenge, and to control my anger. I struggle with wanting to protect. Things do not feel right. I sense an imbalance of feelings that I have never felt before nor had awareness of. I know You're a good God. I know You are a God of justice, goodness, gentleness, graciousness, and mercy. I trust You. I trust that You will bring balance to what is imbalanced. I know You will have order. I know You will make things right.

Give me the strength to trust more. Give me the strength to turn toward You. Give me the gift of faith so that I can take hold of hope. I am fighting at times to believe. Please reassure me that You will make all things right.

Emotional and Spiritual Self-Contemplation

The heightened awareness of the pain of my family and others was so raw at this point in my journey. Even commercials depicting others in pain or need were such a deep trigger. I couldn't watch them. I had to change the channel because I could not contain my deep emotions. I have never in my life felt so emotionally unstable. The obsessive thoughts have now, at this point in my journey, ceased; but they have given way to a wide range of emotions often without warning, filter, or direction. I was out of the denial phase of the stages of grief. I felt like I was emotionally bleeding all over the place. I was irritable, frustrated, sad, and angry. At this place in the journey, I only experienced a fleeting rare moment of peace.

I began to empathize on a whole new level with the pain I saw in others. I so wanted and wished I could end their pain. I wish I could have ended our own. I just had to sit and rest in God's provision and in the gift of peace I knew was to come. That is faith! Waiting for what I was sure of that I saw with my spiritual eyes. Know that your gift of peace is on its way, as well. God is faithful to all and is not a respecter of persons.[10]

I realized we were in good company at this point in our journey. We were in the company of many great men and women in the Bible who waited on God for healing, deliverance, vindication, justice, and peace. I wonder what it must have felt like for Daniel when he was placed in the lion's den.[11] That must have been a very long and unsettling night. But God was faithful as He has always been and the God of Daniel will answer your prayers as well. Stay strong and courageous!

Scriptures

Lamentations 3:25 ESV
The Lord is good to those who wait for him, to the soul who seeks him.

Psalm 27:14 ESV
Wait for the Lord; be strong, and let your heart take courage; wait for the Lord!

Psalm 130:5-6 ESV
I wait for the Lord, my soul waits, and in his word I hope; my soul waits for the Lord more than watchmen for the morning, more than watchmen for the morning

Micah 7:7 ESV
But as for me, I will look to the Lord; I will wait for the God of my salvation; my God will hear me.

Daily Prayer

Lord, thank you for Your word. I hide Your truth deep within my hearts. I claim agreement with it and hope to be renewed by the power of Your word. Thank you for fighting my battles. Thank you for being a God of victory, strength, and mercy. Thank you for the conquering you will do for me. Amen

Prayer Journal Questions

Personal Reflections...
1. What feelings/emotions are you struggling with?   What do you need deliverance from today?
2. How is the suffering of others impacting you today?

3. What is the waiting like today?

4. Describe the ways you are becoming aware of your triggers?

5. What coping behaviors are helping you when you are triggered?

6. What Scriptures are giving you hope?

DAY 9

Throwing in the Towel

"Your attitude towards failure determines your altitude after failure."

- John Maxwell

Praying for the strength to rise up:

This morning is particularly difficult. Forgive me, Lord, I feel like such a failure. This morning feels like a bit of an emotional relapse. I feel like I cannot stand underneath the burden that is on me. I am broken and I feel defeated, attacked in every area of my life. I feel like I can't fight anymore. I feel conquered and defeated. I have nothing left to give.

Everything I do and even in ministry, at this point, now feels like such a burden. It hurts, it hurts so deep. My emotions are raw. I have never felt so conquered in my life. I feel alone, but not abandoned. I sense You, God, but it feels like You're watching me rather than embracing me.

I am not angry at You. I believe being called to ministry is an honor and a gift, but with that comes a great burden and cost. I just don't have the ability to pay that cost today. I beg You for a miracle, without it I cannot go on. The pain and the hurt is so real. I feel incapable of fulfilling what You have called me to do, not just in ministry, but also as a husband and father. I feel inadequate.

I pray that You will lift me up and sustain me. I pray that Your peace will overflow me and my family. I pray blessings on my marriage and that I may be the husband You've called me to be. I pray that I will be faithful, steadfast, *courageous and strong. I realize, though, that none of these come naturally to me and without Your Holy Spirit I am bankrupt. Sustain me, oh God, and make me ever new.*

Emotional and Spiritual Self-Contemplation

Sometimes when we are struggling emotionally and deeply, it impacts the things we loved to do prior to the pain. I just did not have the energy or the desire to engage in things that I once enjoyed like sports, hiking, and fishing. I guess the pain depletes us of any emotional and energy reserves. With no reserves or margins, everything starts to feel like an insurmountable task. I felt this in my calling as a Pastor and in my career as a counselor. If I was totally honest, I felt the same way in my role as a parent and husband. This was a scary and unsettling reality for me. I had nearly zero reserves and was on autopilot just to function. All my energy was redirected to grieving. The problem is the world and its pressures and responsibilities don't make accommodations for our pains. I felt like such a failure.

The morning I wrote this prayer was particularly tough and as I looked toward the Scriptures for hope, answers, or a miracle. I settled on Psalm 88. It validated much of what I was feeling this morning. But my hope was sustained in Him who hears my prayers and yours today. If you're feeling like a failure this morning or totally depleted, be encouraged because your suffering is not in vain. God gives purpose to your suffering. Neither you nor I are failures. We are the beloved of God. We are overcomers and conquerors in Christ Jesus. It is God who measures and determines our worth, values, and defines our identity. You are not a failure, but rather a child of God. God doesn't determine your value based on your biggest mistakes or regrets. He sees you based on the real you He created you to be.

Sometimes even those around us may say things or act in a way that is in contradiction to the truth of Scripture and how God sees us. You can't let this situation or any person steal your identity, worth, or value, all of which are determined by God and God alone.

I often reminded myself of Christ's suffering as He endured the weight of that heavy cross and the march up that hill for your benefit and mine. The weight He bore was the price for the reward. In our suffering we can identify with a Savior who was well acquainted with suffering and can empathize with ours. The weight you bear today you have to believe is proportionate to the reward, renewal, and the miracle that is to come.

Scriptures

2 Corinthians 12:9-10 NIV
But he said to me, "My grace is sufficient for you, for my power is made perfect in weakness." Therefore I will boast all the more gladly of my weaknesses, so that the power of Christ may rest upon me. [10] For the sake of Christ, then, I am content with weaknesses, insults, hardships, persecutions, and calamities. For when I am weak, then I am strong.

Philippians 4:19 ESV
And my God will supply every need of yours according to his riches in glory in Christ Jesus.

Philippians 4:13 ESV
I can do all things through him who strengthens me.

Daily Prayer

Thank You for Your Word. I claim agreement with Your word and will be renewed by it. Thank You for fighting my battles. Thank You for being a God of victory. I am made adequate in Christ Jesus. Amen.

Prayer Journal Questions

Personal Reflections...
1. Describe the ways you felt like you have failed in this journey at any point?
2. Discuss with Jesus how His suffering impacts your perspective of your own suffering?

3. Where is God in your pain?

4. What lies are you struggling with that are in conflict with who God says you are?

5. Identify five Scriptures that address your new identity, worth, and value.

DAY 10

Consuming Fire

"Outside of the cross of Jesus Christ, there is no hope in this world. That cross and resurrection at the core of the Gospel is the only hope for humanity. Wherever you go, ask God for wisdom on how to get that Gospel in, even in the toughest situations of life."

-Ravi Zacharias

Praying through a unrelenting pain:

Lord, this morning my anger is such a consuming fire. If I allow it to consume me, every fiber of my being will burn with rage. It is so tempting. This anger feels justified, appropriate, and called for. Although this may begin as a righteous anger, the sin in me wants to act out. It wants to blame, it wants to settle scores, and it wants vengeance.

In these moments it is difficult to hear You. It's as if I'm alone with an unquenchable fire of anger. In these moments it is difficult to feel You. It's as if all peace in me is lost and hope has fled. I cry and shake terribly, wanting to scream at the top of my lungs. The hole is big, it is dark, and it is deep. It's a place reminiscent of my past. It's ironic, that in the dark pit of rage there's a comfort to it that I used to know. But, I also know it's a place I do not want to revisit. It calls to me in those moments of weakness and desperation. Going to this place is not a sign of victory. For a moment it feels powerful but in the end it leads to feelings of turmoil, pain, and an emotional prison. The devil *wants nothing more than for me to be bloodthirsty for revenge and stuck. This is the distraction he wants for me. To hinder me in actualizing the redemptive purpose God has for my life and the life of my family.*

How can my being stuck help? How can my wanting vengeance bring healing? They are all self-seeking. They are all selfish. They are all empty of God's influence and plan. So, what do I do? I cry for help! I cry out to You, God, loud and hard. I cry out again and again, for I know You hear me and I trust that You will heal me.

Lord, I know You hear me! Lord, I do cry out to You in faith. I intercede for my family. We need You now! We thank You for the comfort that You've granted, for the peace You have provided, and for the healing that has begun. We trust You and Your promises. Only in You can we find hope and healing. Thank You for Your faithfulness. To God be the glory, amen.

Emotional and Spiritual Self-Contemplation

I adopted unbiblical and maladaptive views of anger at various points in life. Between moves and transitions in my life I have been part of various different church cultures as a young man and somehow, they communicated to me that being angry was wrong, and even sinful; at the very least, immature spiritual growth. Yet as I searched Scriptures, I realized anger is a normal emotion and even God has moments of anger. The Scripture says, "Do not sin in your anger."[12] It does not say, "do not be angry." So, I imagine that sinful anger is the result of a self-seeking heart that in its anger is selfish, judging, vengeful, and destructive. When it does not get its way, it produces sinful expressions of anger through its harsh treatment of others.

However, there is a godly anger. I have come to understand this as an anger that is a response to an injustice, un-holiness, pain, hurt, or sin. This type of anger can produce fruit. The fruit produced by this expression of anger is often acts of righteousness and obedience to God. Sometimes our anger can propel much growth. Godly anger can drive things such as charitable giving, supporting those in need, or a commitment to stop human trafficking. It is propelled by a heartfelt desire to act and bring about love and value for the needs of others. We say things like, "Something must be done about this, and I am the one to do it!"

If you reflect over biblical figures or persons in Scripture you will often find that many had moments of anger that led to righteousness and glory to God. We are all familiar with more contemporary figures that experienced righteous anger that led to a fruitful outcome and a Godly result. These individuals would include Mother Theresa, Martin Luther King Jr., and Billy Graham. Even charitable organizations were birthed out of a righteous Godly anger.

For those of you reading this book, it's probably because you are journeying through grief, pain, and sadness. I imagine that at various points on your journey you have felt intense anger—righteous anger. Today, we take a stand against pain and against what the devil meant for destruction. We are angry at loss, death, disease, pain, injury, trauma, and sin. Scripture promises us that God will work all things for good for those who love the Lord.[13] We claim this by faith. If you are not sure what your beliefs are about God, I encourage you to place your trust in Jesus today. It's quite simple. You just need to invite Him into your life as your Savior and the Rescuer of your soul and your pain today.

Scriptures
1 John 4:14-16 (ESV) says,
And we have seen and testify that the Father has sent his Son to be the Savior of the world. Whoever confesses that Jesus is the Son of God, God abides in him, and he in God. So we have come to know and to believe the love that God has for us. God is love, and whoever abides in love abides in God, and God abides in him.

Romans 12:19-21 ESV

Beloved, never avenge yourselves, but leave it to the wrath of God, for it is written, "Vengeance is mine, I will repay, says the Lord." To the contrary, "if your enemy is hungry, feed him; if he is thirsty, give him something to drink; for by so doing you will heap burning coals on his head." Do not be overcome by evil, but overcome evil with good.

Jeremiah 29:11-14 ESV

For I know the plans I have for you, declares the Lord, plans for welfare and not for evil, to give you a future and a hope. Then you will call upon me and come and pray to me, and I will hear you. You will seek me and find me, when you seek me with all your heart. I will be found by you, declares the Lord, and I will restore your fortunes and gather you from all the nations and all the places where I have driven you, declares the Lord, and I will bring you back to the place from which I sent you into exile.

Daily Prayer

Lord if your promises to ancient Israel were as good as we see in Jeremiah 29:11, I am eager for a greater, new covenant promise that can only come through Jesus' perfect work. I stand firm and look forward to it. Amen.

Prayer Journal Questions

Personal Reflections...
1. Is the anger you're experiencing just or unjust?
2. What is your anger compelling you to do?

3. How is it leaning you toward Christ?

4. In what ways is your anger self-seeking? How are you handling self-seeking anger?

5. How are you coping with anger?

DAY 11

━━━━━━ ❧❦❧ ━━━━━━

The Father of Lies

"One of Satan's most deceptive and powerful ways of defeating us is to get us to believe a lie. And the biggest lie is that there are no consequences to our own doing."

- Charles Stanley

Taking back what the devil stole:

This morning, Lord, my thoughts shifted to the cost of a lie and the confusion it causes. A lie robs us of our identity. It's You, Father, that has named us appropriately and called us according to Your will. A lie steals ground; it hurts, and encourages us to give up. The devil is the father of lies. He preys on those called of God to distract them from their redemptive purposes according to the Father's will. I stand this morning and call all lies out to be exposed. I take a stand in Christ Jesus to accept nothing less than truth. I claim truth for my family and I confront all lies that have been competing for truth during this journey of pain. Lies tell us that life will never be good again. Lies tell us it's all our fault. Lies tell us we are on our own. Lies tell us that God has abandoned us.

It is God and God alone who defines our worth and value; it is, You, God, who has called us by our name, and who has chosen our divine destiny. What God has put into motion, no devil or person or trauma or grief can destroy. If You are for us who can be against us?[14]

God, You work all things for good for those who love You. I demand in the name of Christ Jesus that the devil pay back with interest, every bit of ground that he has stolen from us, in the name of Jesus Christ. We have full and complete authority in the name of Jesus Christ to demand such things. That devil, pain, loss, trauma, hurt is obligated to pay up and pay back even more than that which has been stolen. I claim peace. I claim wholeness. I claim restoration. I claim healing. I claim resolution. I claim forgiveness. I claim freedom. I claim truth. I claim God's sovereignty over our lives. I claim all of these good things in the name of Jesus Christ my Lord, for my family. To God be the glory. In the name of Jesus, amen.

Emotional and Spiritual Self-Contemplation

Whenever pain is present, the vulnerability to develop and believe lies are present, as well. Oftentimes, this is influenced by our past experiences or upbringing, or our church family culture. A real enemy also strikes when we are weak and struggling emotionally and spiritually. Thankfully, I am reminded that when we are weak Christ is strong in us.[15]

When we are hurting we struggle with various amounts of guilt and shame. We question if there was anything we could have done to intervene: Could we have stopped it? We question why we did not do more. "If only...." We question our behaviors. We bargain with circumstance. For many of us, the pain goes inward and we point the finger of accusation at ourselves. This is where a lie often takes root.

Such lies that are often developed in the midst of pain are lies surrounding inadequacy, shame, failure, incompetence, and control. We believe we are disappointments. The list of lies we could potentially buy into and believe is miles long. This directly hurts our true identity.

It's only in Christ, that we discover who we really are. This is where we need to take every thought captive and bring it into obedience to Christ and the truth of Scripture. God has given you a name. He calls you His son, His daughter, His precious children. God loves you and He formed your name and identity. So hold on to it and fight off the lies that try to re-label you.

Scriptures

2 Corinthians 5:17 ESV
Therefore, if anyone is in Christ, he is a new creation. The old has passed away; behold, the new has come.

John 10;10 ESV
The thief comes only to steal and kill and destroy. I came that they may have life and have it abundantly.

Matthew 24:4 ESV
And Jesus answered them, "See that no one leads you astray."

1 Peter 5:8 ESV
Be sober-minded; be watchful. Your adversary the devil prowls around like a roaring lion, seeking someone to devour.

Revelation 12:10 ESV
And I heard a loud voice in heaven, saying, "Now the salvation and the power and the kingdom of our God and the authority of his Christ have come, for the accuser of our brothers has been thrown down, who accuses them day and night before our God."

Daily Prayer

I thank You and accept Your Word and promise over my life. It is by no other name that I will experience rest, peace, and rescue. It is by Your stripes that I will be healed. In the name of Jesus, I claim Your promises over my family. Amen.

Prayer Journal Questions

Personal Reflections...
1. Share with God how lies have caused confusion for you at this time. Ask the Holy Spirit to expose those lies and invite the Holy Spirit to show you the truth.

2. What are three tempting lies that you believe about yourself?

3. What is the identity in Scripture that God has given you?

4. How will you know if you received the identity that Christ has given you? What are you going to do differently to claim it in the name of Jesus?

DAY 12

⊷⊶

Renewed Hope

"And you will feel secure, because there is hope;
you will look around and take your rest in security."

- Job 11:18

Finding hope on my Rock:

As I struggle with hope, I find my tolerance of petty things and minor stressors to be lessened. I feel less patient with others. It is a surreal feeling to suffer while the world seems to continue, unaware of our pain. It is not that I want other people to hurt or even know what I'm going through. I do not seek attention, instead I just want the pressure from others to back off. I want the freedom to be able to breathe without everyday pressures. As I grieve, I have little to no accommodations from work, extended family, friends, and the like. It may not be appropriate that any of these people in my environment know what I am feeling. But then how can I expect accommodations if no one knows what I am going through? My mind reasons on a level my emotions cannot. I emotionally want and expect things that my mind tells me are not realistic. Sometimes, I feel the battle between my thinking brain and my emotional brain. I am just tired. You call me to You, Lord. Your yoke is easy and Your burden is light.[16] You call the burdened to Yourself to replace their heavy weights with Your peace.

I thank You for those that You placed in my life that I trust, that I share with, and that I cry with. Still, even at times, I feel triggered by them; and *their expectations that I am doing better; expectations that things are OK; expectations that this is just a short season of pain. You know my heart. You know that my emotions vacillate between extremes, sometimes moment to moment, hour to hour, and day to day. Those that I share with have great intentions and hopes. They want us to be better and they want us to do better "now!" I realize sometimes their comments are more for their own comfort than for ours. They want to support but maybe they're uncomfortable with the grieving process. Maybe they feel ill-equipped. Maybe it's just that they can't make it better. Only You can make it better. You are making it better. You are my "all in all." You're more than enough for me. My problems do not get old for You nor do they bore You. I know that You care deeply for me and my family and what our hearts feel. Those that are close to us, mean well and I accept and appreciate their best efforts. They are only a complement to You and Your work. I acknowledge that You placed them in my life for added support and love; but it is by and through Your hand alone that we will have reprieve and rest.*

I am tired. I feel tired and I am tired of people, at times. But this feeling I know is only for this moment. So it is OK, as I know it will pass. I cannot depend on my own feelings for they are ever changing, like the wind. What is unchanging is the Rock on which I stand; what is unchanging is that You are my strong fortress; what is unchanging is You. I hold on to faith in the God who does not change, in the God who is stable, in the God who is trustworthy, in the God who is faithful, in the God who is our Deliver, in the God who is our Rock and Shelter. Thank You for being stable when I am not. You are so comforting.

Emotional and Spiritual Self-Contemplation

Was it not just yesterday that I felt more hopeful, stronger, and more certain of what truth is? How interesting this journey is, that in such a short period of time my emotions can fluctuate so much. I thank God that truth is not dependent on my emotions or how I feel. My feelings are rapidly and ever changing. Feelings are like the wind or the tides of the ocean; they come and go, they vary in intensity, and they are never predictable. No matter what you're feeling today just know that truth is based on the Word of God and not the ever-changing emotions of this journey. There is a stabilizing truth that will ground you and keep you. Don't ever become a salesman to yourself and buy the rationalization. Although our feelings mean something and are valuable, truth never originated with feelings nor is truth influenced by feelings.

Truth stands all by itself. It doesn't need someone to rationalize it, explain it, or try to sell it. The truth may be hard and difficult to accept, but it is stable, transcendent, and unchanging. We only talk ourselves into bad ideas. I am thankful that for me truth is found in God's promises. I am reminded of that amazing moment in Luke 2 when the angel announced to Mary that she would have a son that was everyone's answer to prayer and need. As she struggled to comprehend all that was being announced to her the angel reminded her that, "every promise of God will never fail." What an amazing truth to put your trust in despite the ever changing tides of emotions.

Hope was nearly absent for me when I was compelled to write this. I noticed that on days where feelings of hope were fleeting, my emotional tolerance ranged from minimal to non-existent. I was frustrated, angry, irritable and tough to be around. I found that with hope came life and with the absence of hope only despair and negativity remained. Hope is a gift from God. When it felt distant, I felt cursed. Absence of hope is like a curse.

The story of Job gave me hope this morning. Job persevered through such deep loss and pain. Remember, Job is a man who lost it all. In one day he lost all of his ten children and all his riches. He was tested and broken. But, like Job, if we remain faithful and press through in prayer we will meet God on this journey like we would never have imagined. Like Job, who journeyed bruised and battered, you will have a newfound hope in God and His promises. God restored Job beyond his imagination and He is faithful to do the same for us today.

Scriptures

Romans 8:38-39 NIV

For I am convinced that neither death nor life, neither angels nor demons, neither the present nor the future, nor any powers, neither height nor depth, nor anything else in all creation, will be able to separate us from the love of God that is in Christ Jesus our Lord.

Romans 15:13 ESV

May the God of hope fill you with all joy and peace in believing, so that by the power of the Holy Spirit you may abound in hope.

James 1:12 NIV

Blessed is the one who perseveres under trial because, having stood the test, that person will receive the crown of life that the Lord has promised to those who love him.

Daily Prayer

Thank you for the gift of hope. My hope is renewed daily by You. I abide in Your promises of life and abundance. You are the God of my destiny as long as You are present in my life. Hope is a gift to be celebrated for all time. Hope is never-ending. Amen.

Prayer Journal Questions

Personal Reflections...
1. In moments where hope seems lost, how has it impacted your thinking, behaviors, and faith?
2. How is hope important to you while on this leg of your journey?

3. At this point in the journey, what truth do you struggle with?

4. What hope are you asking God for or what hope has to be renewed?

DAY 13

❦

Loneliness Battle

*"Snuggle in God's arms. When you are hurting, when you feel
lonely, left out. Let Him cradle you, comfort you,
reassure you of His all-sufficient power and love."*

- Kay Arthur

Prayer of assurance that I am not alone:

Dear God, last night I could not shake the utter darkness and isolation of
feeling lonely. I don't know what it is about me or maybe what's broken in
me, but there are more times than not where I feel utterly and completely alone.
I know You are always there and it's not that I feel like You have abandoned
me. It's that I sometimes feel disconnected, especially now, with all this pain.
But it's not only from You; it's from everyone. Sadly, this is not a new feeling for
me, as I have felt this way as a child. I guess the current pain has brought out
and deepened what has always been residing inside me. It used to frighten me.

Throughout my life I've learned to fill that hole, more times than not, with
some unhealthy coping mechanisms. I used to run to eating, spending, buying,
almost anything in an attempt to alleviate the fears and anxieties that plagued
me. They all came up empty. That's what counterfeits do. They over promise and
underdeliver and they keep you stuck longer than you can ever imagine. As a
believer, I try to fill that hole with You and the peace You provide, but there are
times I am just completely broken.

What is wrong with me? This evening we had an amazing worship service and yet I asked myself: "How can I be in an environment surrounded by hundreds of people in worship and still feel utterly and completely disconnected from everyone?" My face is inviting. I even play the part, but deep inside, You know what I feel. I'm grieving and I'm hurting. "Fake it 'til you make it," I tell myself, but I have not made it yet. Not sure how long I can keep waiting. The good thing is that I like my self-care time by myself. I like to take time to work on projects and not be bothered by anyone; but feeling lonely is scary and painful.

It's difficult to talk to others about my feelings. I recognize that my feelings of loneliness are no one's fault. There is no lack of love, friendship, or people in my life. Actually, I probably have more people in my life whom I do life with than most. I am blessed and fortunate. Nevertheless, something in me is broken.

Certainly my brokenness does not shock You, for You knew me before I was conceived and yet You chose my existence. You are God, the Creator of all things and You choose to be concerned for me.

Although I feel lonely, I am not alone, for You are with me. The many blessings, the people that You have put in my life stand with me, as well. I thank You for my wife and her love. I thank You for my children and the joy they bring to me. I thank You for my church family and the life that they bring. I declare Your Word with my lips. I claim it over my life and the freedom that it brings. My tongue brings forth life or death and today I choose life! I speak the blessings of Your Word over my life.

Emotional and Spiritual Self-Contemplation

It is both ironic and tragic that in a time where we are more connected with technology than ever, we also see some of the highest recorded rates of loneliness in history. Loneliness is an emotional state in which we feel isolated or completely alone in the world. Loneliness often has little to do with being with people, as we can feel lonely even when surrounded by others. Lonely is about feeling detached, unknown and distant from others. Loneliness does not depend on how many friends or relationships you have but rather on subjective feelings and beliefs about your relationships.

It's interesting how situations like this can pull out past baggage and pain that have been buried for years. An important truth is this: What is buried never really dies. It will chase after you and you will take it with you everywhere you go and into every relationship. God used this very real feeling of being "lonely" in my journey to highlight an area of my healing that I have always needed but somehow suppressed, neglected, ignored or long forgot. Somehow, this current pain has become a catalyst for a positive change in my life. My current pain was the doorway to the healing of my past pain.

I began to learn a lot about myself and I learned that feeling lonely was not that I was actually alone, but rather, I didn't know how to accurately express all that was going on inside of me, leaving me feeling unknown and misunderstood by others. Perhaps this was due to a lack of skills I never learned or maybe I just didn't take the time to try. So, through the work of the Holy Spirit, I began to see what was broken and a process of inner healing and confidence in sharing my emotions, first with God, then with others, began.

Scriptures

Isaiah 41:10 ESV
Fear not, for I am with you; be not dismayed, for I am your God; I will strengthen you, I will help you, I will uphold you with my righteous right hand.

Romans 8:35-39 ESV
Who shall separate us from the love of Christ? Shall tribulation, or distress, or persecution, or famine, or nakedness, or danger, or sword? As it is written, "For your sake we are being killed all the day long; we are regarded as sheep

to be slaughtered." No, in all these things we are more than conquerors through him who loved us. For I am sure that neither death nor life, nor angels nor rulers, nor things present nor things to come, nor powers, nor height nor depth, nor anything else in all creation, will be able to separate us from the love of God in Christ Jesus our Lord.

1 Samuel 12:22 ESV
For the Lord will not forsake his people, for his great name's sake, because it has pleased the Lord to make you a people for himself.

Daily Prayer

Lord, I pray that You would allow each of us in our journeys to experience Your presence and comfort. Feeling alone is so difficult. I thank You for Your promises and the guarantee of Your presence in my life. To God be the glory. Amen.

Prayer Journal Questions

Personal Reflections...
1. How is God using your journey to show you things about yourself?
2. What past wounds are being brought to the surface that you may have not been aware of?

3. Use an emotional language in your journaling to express all that you feel today. When it comes to being a good listener, God has all the time you need.

4. What inner work is taking place in you or have you asked God to begin?

DAY 14

Tired...Exhausted

"We are starved for quiet, to hear the sound of sheer silence that is the presence of God himself."

- Ruth Haley Barton

Prayer for strength in this journey:

Father, I am tired. Today is one of those days when I am feeling the weight of everything. I feel like everything is crashing down on me all at once, and my normal tolerance to it is absent. I am tired. I'm exhausted. I want to rest. Chaos is not ensuing around me, but it feels like it is. A lot of little things happened today and they are all piling up fast. Did I mention I am tired? Tears consume my eyes and my chest is weighted. It's hard to breathe. I know I am being attacked by the enemy and many other things in life. There is no escaping my feelings today. Nevertheless, I hope in You. You are the only direction I can run to. You are the only fortress and stronghold for me. I pray for immediate deliverance. I need it now!

I question how much more I can tolerate. Yes, I have felt this way before, and You continue to give me the strength to endure. Just when I think I can't take anymore, just when I think I'm going to crack, You are there. I look forward to the night to come. I look forward to resting my head. I want to sleep. I hope to wake up tomorrow renewed. I want it so desperately to be a new day.

Emotional and Spiritual Self-Contemplation

What I was feeling that night was intense anxiety and panic. During my emotional recovery journey, I had this same experience a handful of times. It was often the result of allowing my thoughts to become negative and run wild without boundaries. I gave way to these intensified feelings by giving my mind over to them and not abiding in God's Word as self-care for my soul and emotions. Just as our tongue can bring life and death, so can our thoughts. Thoughts are the voice of the soul and how we think will often dictate how we feel. This can be either so wonderful or terrible based on the nature of our thought lives.

I learned a key to spiritual self-care in responding to these moments. I began to practice solitude and quietness before the Lord, often meditating on areas of Scripture that spoke to or shed light on my current needs and emotional state. I also used Scripture to correct negative thinking and the temptation to think negatively, much like Jesus did in the desert when He was fasting, and Satan tried to tempt Him.[17] Jesus responded to lies and temptation with the Word of truth and so can we. We must!

Scriptures

1 Corinthians 10:13 ESV

No temptation has overtaken you that is not common to man. God is faithful, and he will not let you be tempted beyond your ability, but with the temptation he will also provide the way of escape, that you may be able to endure it.

Matthew 11:28 ESV

Come to me, all who labor and are heavy laden, and I will give you rest.

Isaiah 40:31 ESV

but they who wait for the Lord shall renew their strength;
    they shall mount up with wings like eagles;
they shall run and not be weary;
    they shall walk and not faint.

Daily Prayer

Lord, I pray for emotional and spiritual rest and renewal. May my heavy heart feel protected and sustained by You. Lift me up and bring me rest in Your perfect peace. Amen

Prayer Journal Questions

Personal Reflections...
1. Share with the Lord the heaviness of your heart.
2. What negative thoughts have you allowed to run wild without boundaries?

3. How can you engage Scripture to address your thought patterns?

4. How can Scripture memorization help you? Which is a stabilizing rock for you?

5. Discuss with God the comfort you are in need of today.

DAY OF REST

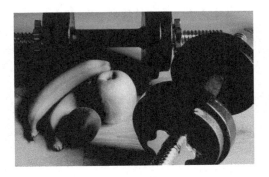

This journey of grief and the losses of many types often feels like it has sabotaged our lives. It feels like an invader that has broken through our lines and stops us in our tracks. Life as we have known it often comes to a crashing standstill, or at least it feels that way. For today's day of rest, I want to encourage you to take back what is yours. There is an encouraging Scripture I often stand on which reminds me that I will be restored in an even greater amount. "But if he (thief) is caught, he will pay sevenfold; he will give all the goods of his house."[18] Whatever it is that you feel has been taken from you trust that God will restore it back to you in even a greater measure.

Let's take a step of faith today. Change your routine. Go out and treat yourself. Whether you're like me and you find rest and rejuvenation in nature or maybe it's over a meal with friends. Pick that special activity that suits you best and enjoy it.

Today can also be a day of great empowerment for you. Do something that makes you feel good about you. Maybe you haven't been to the gym in a while, went out to your favorite café, watch your favorite movie, spend the day at the spa or whatever it is that makes you feel good about you. For a short time let it take you away from your pain for a little while. Have fun with it.

DAY 15

Let's Make a Deal

*"The irony is that while God doesn't need us but still wants us,
we desperately need God but don't really want Him most of the time."*

- Francis Chan

Prayer for trading my sorrows:

Lord, as you know, I haven't been myself for a couple of weeks. When I first realized the feelings of losing myself, I thought I would wake up the next morning and return back to my normal self. Well, it's been weeks and I still feel disconnected. I find myself caring about things less and less. I just don't care. My tolerance to issues continues to be nearly absent. All I want is full recovery. I want what was stolen replaced. It is hard for me to dream. It is difficult to dream of a recovered life after loss. I struggle to imagine how things can be OK again.

It is so hard to find joy in other things. When joy is there, it is only there for a fleeting moment. When I feel joy for those brief moments, it is followed by exhaustion. I become emotionally drained and empty inside. My challenge is that after experiencing fleeting moments of joy I am reminded of who I used to be. I miss who I was before loss, pain, and hurt. Life felt safe and stable. I was happy. This realization is followed by guilt. I feel guilty that I took those moments for granted. I did not fully appreciate what I had. It took such a deep loss for me to realize how wonderful those moments were. I wish I could have *them back. Why didn't I realize the value earlier? There is so much I would do differently. Oh God, forgive me for bargaining!*

I feel so desperate wishing I had a do-over, a chance to go back and do things differently. My eyes fill with tears now as I realize that I blame myself!

I know I am not responsible for the situation that I find myself in today, but could there have been something that I could have done? Could I have intervened? Could I have changed things? Could I have made different decisions? Why?

These are such difficult feelings to bear. I have never felt such deep pain.

I feel like I have been lost in this process of grief for far too long. I cannot control nor manage it. Where will I be in the end? Where will my family be? Will we even get there?

I will commit to renewing my mind with Your Word. I ask You to rebuild. I ask You to redeem. I lay my guilt and my shame at the foot of Your cross. May my conscience not bear witness against me, but may I accept the washing of Your blood and grace. Lord, I trust that You will do what I am powerless to do. Amen.

Emotional and Spiritual Self-Contemplation

As I reflected back over this prayer, it was difficult to read and connect again with these feelings. Looking back, I found myself camped out at this point in my journey for weeks. This prayer really captured for me the desperation that is grief, as well as the journey. It can be terrible when all of the feelings and thoughts heighten and hit you at once. God is the only direction we can go to for relief. I found validation in Psalm 69 as the psalmist really captured my emotions. It was like reading my own emotional story.

The anger, at this turn in the journey, was so deep and raw. It was like an anger of rage and desperation to repay evil with justice. Scripture says, "Vengeance is the Lord's," but in my anger I wanted vengeance to be mine. I did not act on my anger outwardly. However, I did in my heart. My anger would often take on a life of its own. I felt rage. The pressure would be so high at times that I scared myself. I never knew it was possible to be so angry. I was bargaining with God; what was, what used to be; and I bargained with myself.

I grappled with the deepest of self-blame. I didn't directly blame myself, but rather found myself blaming, in my bargaining and questioning. I wanted to intervene, to change circumstances, to alter events, but I could not. This is where my self-blame took root; it was in my inability to alter events. With this came unrealistic expectations. I was expecting that somehow I should have known or foreseen what was to occur and intervene to stop it and protect. I know now that this thinking was so unrealistic and unhealthy; but at the time, it was my way of processing and grieving my pain. I bargained and resisted to accept the reality of my situation.

Strangely, I also found myself encouraged that I was not alone and neither are you today. There are many biblical figures that struggled with pain, grief and deep sorrow. David was often troubled and in despair. Many of his psalms describe deep anguish, fears, loneliness, guilt, shame, bargaining, and grief. Jeremiah was known as the weeping prophet. King Solomon wrote Ecclesiastes, and on and on. Jesus Himself, in Isaiah 53:3 says, He was despised and rejected by men, a man of sorrows and acquainted with grief; and as one from whom men hide their face, He was despised, and we esteemed Him not." I was clearly not alone, while on this leg of my journey while in the depths of sorrow; and neither are you alone today. The following Scripture verses gave me so much hope. They were a lifeline.

Scriptures
Psalm 34:22 ESV
The Lord redeems the life of his servants;
   none of those who take refuge in him will be condemned.

Romans 8:1 ESV
There is therefore now no condemnation for those who are in Christ Jesus.

Psalm 147:3 ESV
He heals the brokenhearted
and binds up their wounds.

Matthew 5:4 ESV
Blessed are those who mourn, for they shall be comforted.

Daily Prayer

Lord, I claim these blessings over each of our journeys. I thank You that there is no condemnation, shame or guilt in You. I stand strong on putting on my new identity in Christ. To God be the glory. Amen.

Prayer Journal Questions

Personal Reflections...
1. How do you relate with the depth of emotions you have felt to the many biblical figures that have come before you?
2. How have you experienced bargaining with your circumstances, with God, and within yourself?

3. Share what guilt you may be experiencing. Are you self-blaming?

4. Describe the moments that you have felt lost in the thoughts or pain?

5. What ways have you been able to cope with similar feelings?

DAY 16

⸙

Invisible Pain

"When we deny our pain, losses, and feelings year after year, we become less and less human. We transform slowly into empty shells with smiley faces painted on them... I soon realized that a failure to appreciate the biblical place of feelings within our larger Christian lives has done extensive damage, keeping free people in Christ in slavery."

- Peter Scazzero

Prayer for exposing the lie:

Lord, today I find myself angry at the church. Maybe it's the cultures that we have created regarding pain, sorrow, and grief. Though You make room for these feelings, many church cultures do not. Could it be because these are feelings we would rather avoid? Or is it because of our own ignored wounds, insecurities, and anxieties? Maybe it's the fear of not being able to provide adequate support. Our cultures, at times, avoid these topics and set the expectation that hopefully, it will just go away.

So, I am angry at the church. I'm angry with church leaders and the countless generations before me. I am angry that they made no room for my emotions. I am angry about the broken promises and the broken encouragement to deny my humanity. I received the message to rejoice and be glad and not feel pain. But this isn't real life.

I was taught through culture to feel shame about any pain, sadness, and hurt that I may have been feeling. I am mad that I was told that I should have prayed harder, or that maybe I was in sin, or I didn't give my feelings to God. I am saddened by how many years I lived with guilt and shame, feeling inadequate before God, before the church, and as a human. Some modeled that feeling hurt, sadness, and pain was weakness and not godly. What a lie.

I am tired of being sold half-truths and lies. I don't need anyone to speak for God on behalf of my pain and humanity. The Bible speaks for You, God — it's Your spoken Word. I don't need someone to tell me to name it and claim it or make me guarantees based on my works. Forgive me, God, for unknowingly perpetuating such a culture that does not make room for a person's suffering. I realize now that this is not biblical nor is it the Gospel message. Thank You, Jesus, for making room for my pain and suffering. May I make the same room for others.

Emotional and Spiritual Self-Contemplation

It was while as a Pastor facing my own pain, that I came to see what the Holy Spirit exposed to be an unhealthy church culture that has not made room for those who are hurting—the exact people Jesus' ministry came to save and heal.

What we perceive to be blessings, is actually narrow and limited. Sometimes what we perceive and what God perceives are two very different things. God is true and every man is a liar. Sometimes what God may see as a blessing, we may see as discomfort.

What if God allows us to go through pain because He will leverage it for growth in our lives, for the growth of His kingdom, for His glory's sake? What if a greater good is to come out of a deeper pain? Would our pain, sorrow and discomfort then be good?

You can't promise me that I'm going to have a financial blessing or have my bills paid or doors open for the next opportunity the way I understand those things to come. What if God allows me to struggle to teach me, to correct me, to grow me?

Of course, I believe and it's clear in Scripture that it is God's desire to bless us; but it is also true that our sight and understanding is limited. It says in Deuteronomy 29:29, *"The secret things belong to the Lord our God, but the things revealed belong to us and to our children forever, that we may follow all the words of this law."*

Jesus Himself despaired in the Garden. David was fighting for his life in a cave. Sampson's eyes were gouged out. Job lost everything. Sarah regretted her decision and felt jealousy and anger. Jacob played favorites with his children and created resentment and pain. Cain killed Abel. Jacob lied and hurt Esau. Paul sat in prison, was shipwrecked, starved, and stoned, and even despaired at life while on a missions trip in Asia. All of the apostles, except for one, John, were persecuted for their faith. Somehow, God allowed such things and still allows pain today. But God is a good God. God walks us through the pain. It's often through pain that we grow.

You are created in the image of God. God is not surprised by your feelings and emotions. God is not threatened by your feelings and emotions. Actually, if you are created in the image of God, your sadness, hurt, and pain are feelings that God has felt. What I do with my feelings will either bring glory to God or lead to sin.

Experiencing sadness, hurt, and pain is not an expression of lack of faith; rather, the denying of your humanity and feelings is a lack of faith. I refuse to feel guilty and shame for my feelings. God did not create me to experience guilt and shame. God created us to have a full range of feelings and He is the only source of our healing. It is through the pain that my relationship with God has grown and He has become more real to me.

I am saddened by the history of church leaders who ran from their own feelings and have taught others to do the same. I am saddened that many church leaders have missed it. Facing our feelings and owning them and bringing them to Christ will allow us to experience the fullness of God's love. The nakedness of our emotions before God allows us to truly know Him and be known by Him.

Knowing that Jesus redeems my soul. Allowing myself to be loved by Jesus redeems my life and identity as it is here on earth. He redeems our emotions, as well. We all have a God-sized hole in our lives and in our hearts that only the love of Jesus can fill; not in some counterfeit or shallow way, but in a deep way that is accepting and embracing.

It is my prayer that the church reflects on how they approach emotions. It is my hope that church leaders will be courageous enough to allow themselves to own and deal with their own feelings, emotions. and brokenness, in a God honoring, honest way. Leaders need to encourage and teach others to do the same. As a Pastor and counselor, my pain has taught me much. I make a commitment going forward to create an honest biblical culture that makes room for pain and hurting people. At some point, everyone will face this dark night of the soul and my hope is that churches would actively create a culture that Christ handed to us.

Scriptures
Romans 12:15 ESV
Rejoice with those who rejoice, weep with those who weep.

1 Peter 3:8 ESV
Finally, all of you, have unity of mind, sympathy, brotherly love, a tender heart, and a humble mind.

1 Corinthians 12:25-26 ESV
That there may be no division in the body, but that the members may have the same care for one another. If one member suffers, all suffer together; if one member is honored, all rejoice together.

Daily Prayer

Lord, help me to release my anger and resentments. I lay them down now at the foot of the cross. May I not pick them back up. Grant me perfect peace and love. Amen.

Prayer Journal Questions

Personal Reflections...
1. Have you adopted false beliefs about emotions from others?
2. How did your family deal with hurt and pain?

3. What walls do you put up in hopes of protecting yourself from what you are feeling?

4. How do you feel God sees your pain?

5. How do you find validation in response to biblical figures that have felt pain, as well?

_____

_____

_____

_____

_____

_____

_____

_____

_____

_____

DAY 17

———— ⟋⟍ ————

Missed the Mark

"Lower your expectations of earth;
This isn't heaven, so don't expect it to be."

- Max Lucado

Prayer for everyone who dropped the ball:

Lord, I continue to feel alone often. Not from You, but from others. I feel like those around me who have not experienced what my family has experienced just don't get it. How could they get it? They have not experienced what we have. So, I show them grace, but it is frustrating because I want more. It's not that I necessarily want just more support from them. I just want the right kind of support.

It is frustrating when I hear, "I will pray for you" or "I will keep that in prayer," or "I will add that to my prayer list." Of course many throw in, "Trust in God" or "God will get you through."

I don't want them to pray for me alone. I want them to pray with me, with my family. I want them to join in with me, in my suffering. I do not want them to feel my pain, but I want to see and feel their support in a way that I know they understand me. Their comments feel so minimizing. I feel brushed off and devalued. I feel patronized and pushed aside. Of course I need prayer. Of course I want them to remember me and my family. I need them, those that love us, to stand with us. I want them to stand in the gap when my knees are too weak *to stand, when my voice is too choked up to pray, when I am in such pain that I just need a hug.*

This is what makes us feel so abandoned, the feeling that those around us just want us to rush to get better. Maybe they can't tolerate where we are emotionally right now. Maybe they don't know what to do.

I realize I have done this, too. I have done this to others at various points in my life. Forgive me, God, for being insensitive to their needs. Forgive me, God, for being too absorbed with myself, with life, and with the wrong things. Forgive me, God, for not mourning with those who mourn. If this situation, if this prayer has taught me anything, it has taught me how to stand with those who are in need. It has taught me how to mourn with those that mourn. I understand now the purpose and value of being emotionally and spiritually present. I now get how it is medicine for the heart and the soul. I now get why You call us, as believers, to do this for each other. I never again want to dismiss the pain of another. May the Holy Spirit equip me to show Your love and affection to those in need. May we find comfort in the support of those that You sent to us. I pray that they stand with us, that they join us, that they strengthen us, and that they love us through this.

Emotional and Spiritual Self-Contemplation

As I reflected over this prayer I realized just how lonely this journey felt at times. I recognized that I wanted or maybe needed more than my friends and family were capable of or able to give. I came to understand what I needed most and it was often just a silent emotionally engaged presence. I didn't want someone trying to fix the situation, fix me, or make it better. I knew no one could make it better. It was just an emotional journey of healing. I just wanted someone to walk on the painful journey with me.

As I contemplate loneliness, I think of the prophet Jeremiah. He experienced a very difficult life of loneliness and the deepest rejection. Jeremiah's ministry made him an unpopular person. Actually, he was the spokesman sent to call God's people out on their sins and warn them of judgment, calamity, and disaster, all because of the people's rebellion. He was not the guy that was invited over for dinner, to say the least. He was hated and threatened with death. If this wasn't bad enough, Jeremiah 16:1-2 says, "The word of the Lord came to me: 'You shall not take a wife, nor shall you have sons or daughters in this place'." Talk about experiencing loneliness! He would never know the pleasure of a deep intimate relationship with a spouse or children. Somehow this prophet endured the pain. I imagine what kept him going was the comfort of knowing that he was serving God. It may not have been an emotional comfort, but certainly a spiritual comfort to get him through the loneliest of times.

You see, I have come to understand through this journey that others are not the source of my needs. God alone is my "All in All," He is the "Great I Am." He alone is the source of my hope, peace, joy, contentment, purpose, destiny, and my calling. So what is the purpose of others in my life? They are gifts from God, but they are never greater than the Gift Giver. They are gifts to be enjoyed and do life with. They are there to compliment His love. They are gifts that can never overshadow the greatness of God and all He is to us.

So, as you walk forward today just know that He is your "All in All", He is your "Great I Am." He will meet your needs fully and completely. Let's let those in our lives off the hook and just enjoy them for what they are—gifts to be enjoyed! No one has been put in your life to be the source of your needs. Keep journeying forward. Don't stop journeying, don't stop worshiping, and most of all, don't stop praying. What does Your word have for me today?

Scriptures

Philippians 4:19 ESV

And my God will supply every need of yours according to his riches in glory in Christ Jesus.

Psalm 37:4 ESV
Delight yourself in the Lord, and he will give you the desires of your heart.

Philippians 4:11-12 ESV
Not that I am speaking of being in need, for I have learned in whatever situation I am to be content. I know how to be brought low, and I know how to abound. In any and every circumstance, I have learned the secret of facing plenty and hunger, abundance and need.

2 Corinthians 9:9-11 ESV
As it is written, "He has distributed freely, he has given to the poor; his righteousness endures forever." He who supplies seed to the sower and bread for food will supply and multiply your seed for sowing and increase the harvest of your righteousness. You will be enriched in every way to be generous in every way, which through us will produce thanksgiving to God.

Daily Prayer

Lord, feeling alone is such a terrible emotion to experience. I pray that I would be fully convinced of Your love and promises. Thank you for reminding me that You are with me. Please draw to me as I draw near to You. Amen

Prayer Journal Questions

Personal Reflections...
1. Describe the loneliness you have felt.
2. What expectations have you placed on others that is not their intended responsibility?

3. What does it mean for God to be your "All in ALL," and the "Great I Am"?

4. How can we go about getting our needs met from God?

DAY 18

———— ❧ ————

Hiding in the Shadows

"At the root of all experiences of shame is the sense that we have been exposed and uncovered."

- David Wells[19]

Prayer to stand tall, stand strong:

It occured to me that I have been very busy lately. Too busy to hear, too busy to feel, too busy to think. Am I stuffing my feelings and not dealing with them? Am I running? The answer to my questions is, yes, but not purposefully. It's cool to act like I'm not hurting; to lie to myself that nothing has happened. But, the truth knows all too well. I find that my very being gravitates toward not dealing with things. What would happen if my feelings did not hide in the shadows? I would hurt, I would feel, I would be in need and I would be exposed.

I trust You God, that the process of healing has begun. I see and feel glimpses of it. I know You are faithful to finish the good work You have started. I find my feelings hiding in the shadows with others, too. I don't want them to know. Not because I fear what they would know, but rather because I don't want to explain. It's a painful story. My heart does not want to keep telling it over and over. It may not be wise to tell everyone, but my feelings even hide in the shadows from those that already know. I don't want them to know I'm still hurting. But why? I just want to feel normal again. I know nothing is perfect, and that perfection in this life is not possible.

I realize that I am not the only one hurting. Some are hurting because I'm hurting. It's because they love me. Others are hurting due to their own pains that are separate from my own. What's normal is that we are all in need; in need of a Savior that makes all things new; in need of peace, in need of rescue, and in need of protection. God, You can do all of these things. I place my trust and hope in You. What hope is there to suffer without God? I don't know how others can survive pain without acknowledging the God who can heal and restore. God, I trust in You for what You can do that I cannot. What life can be inspired in me through Your word?

Emotional and Spiritual Self-Contemplation

As I contemplate a day in the shadows, I remember a small, often overlooked story in the book of Numbers. This is a story of a man named Micah and a young Levite that became his priest. This is not a long story and some would say there is not much to be said about it other than Micah felt blessed and that God's favor was now with him because he had his own Levite priest living with him, directing him, and interceding for him. This reminds me that we have, unlike Micah, a permanent priest that continually and forever intercedes for us. His name is Jesus. Micah's priest was of human origin alone and could only intercede for him in a very limited way. In contrast, our Jesus is a High Priest forever who fully understands us and knows us better then we know ourselves.[20]

When I'm hiding in the shadows, this comforts me because I didn't even know what to pray for or I was disconnected with my journey, as a defense mechanism not to deal, cope or feel. Yet my High Priest was faithfully praying and interceding for me even when I no longer was. Jesus is your permanent High Priest, as well. Now this truth brings some real hope. Know that He is fighting for you even when you feel you have no fight left. He is carrying you on this journey even when you feel you can't take another step. He is praying for you even if you have stopped. He is permanent and faithful. Micah' priest was with him for a short season. Our

High Priest Jesus is with us forever. When you are hiding in the shadows, your High Priest isn't, instead, He is at work right now on your behalf.

Scriptures

Hebrews 4:15 ESV

For we do not have a high priest who is unable to sympathize with our weaknesses, but one who in every respect has been tempted as we are, yet without sin.

Hebrews 7:23-27 ESV

The former priests were many in number, because they were prevented by death from continuing in office, but he holds his priesthood permanently, because he continues forever. Consequently, he is able to save to the uttermost[a] those who draw near to God through him, since he always lives to make intercession for them.

For it was indeed fitting that we should have such a high priest, holy, innocent, unstained, separated from sinners, and exalted above the heavens. He has no need, like those high priests, to offer sacrifices daily, first for his own sins and then for those of the people, since he did this once for all when he offered up himself.

Daily Prayer

Lord, I claim these blessings over each of our journeys. I celebrate that You are my high priest that is always without fail covering me with your love and protection. To God be the glory. Amen.

Prayer Journal Questions

Personal Reflections...
1. What have you done when you found yourself hiding in the shadows on your journey?
2. What things have you occupied yourself with in an attempt to not feel, cope, or deal with your feelings?

3. Have you found it difficult to pray?

4. What does it mean to you or what comfort do you find in a High Priest who intercedes continually on your behalf?

DAY 19

Your Name is Victory

"Taste and see that the Lord is good;
blessed is the one who takes refuge in him."

- Psalm 34:8

Prayer for a joy no circumstance can steal:

Lord, the first celebratory moment on this journey has come and gone. A birthday! I am writing this prayer as I was lamenting while eating a piece of the birthday cake. Birthdays and cakes are such a time of celebration. They are synonymous with love, joy, positivity, and optimism. It is an interesting feeling though, approaching this level of celebration while my heart is still not emotionally present. At first, I felt detached and frustrated. I was angry that I could not be emotionally present in this moment for my daughter. Frustrated that I could not emotionally experience for myself the celebration and joy I remembered at moments like this.

Thankfully, the Holy Spirit intervened and I heard that small voice. I then had a perspective shift. As I looked at the cake it became for me a reminder of the stabilizing truth of the joy that is in Christ. A peace that surpasses understanding. That I can have joy even in the midst of suffering. Joy and happiness are not the same thing. Happiness is a fleeting feeling that always changes. But joy is a sustaining inner attribute of God. True joy only comes from knowing You God, and being known by You. This cake reminds me of joy.

It reminded me of the spirit within me, the Holy Spirit. It also reminds me of the assurances of Your promises. This is a sweet cookies and cream birthday cake. In my pain, I received more out of this particular birthday cake than I have ever received in my life with all of the birthday cakes combined. Somehow, in my pain God, You grabbed a hold of something deep within me today. Thank You.

Emotional and Spiritual Self-Contemplation

A few days later, after having eaten all the leftover cake, something deep in my soul continued to stir. I felt compelled to claim something new by faith. I sat my wife and kids down and asked them if they wanted to celebrate again and have another cake. Of course they said, "Yes!" So, I went further and explained that this was not an ordinary cake but that this was a cake of victory and faith. I then set out to the store and bought another cookies and cream cake. When the baker asked me whose name to put on the cake, I responded, "Victory!" She said, "What a lovely name!" I agreed. However, I was too emotional to tell her that it was not the name of a person, but the name of a promise.

If a birthday cake represents a celebration, what this cake represented to my family was far more. Upon it you would have noticed the word "Victory" because it was ours. We proclaimed it in the partaking of this cake. We had faith for the victory that was ours that day and the days to follow. Things were very hard on us as a family. Each of us was dealing with the pain in different ways but we claimed the same victory. That day we took a stand against pain and against what the devil meant for destruction. Scripture promises us that God will work all things for good for those who love the Lord.[21] We are all lovers of God in my house. So again, we claimed His promise by faith.

My wife, myself and our four children took the opportunity to blow out a candle. Blowing out the candle represented us saying that the bondage, the fire of pain, and wounds no longer had control over us. We cancelled it out in the name of Christ. At that moment, we claimed to be set free in Christ Jesus.

What a powerful moment that was. Something shifted in that exercise of faith. Though it was a figurative exercise, it was also profoundly spiritual. I was reminded what faith was; the full confidence of what I was believing God for, and the absolute unwavering belief that it would happen. We claimed something new that day and had no doubt God was going to respond. Our beliefs were so strong that we considered it already done and celebrated it with a cake.

Scriptures

Numbers 6:24-26 ESV
The Lord bless you and keep you;
the Lord make his face to shine upon you and be gracious to you;
the Lord lift up his countenance[a] upon you and give you peace.

Hebrews 11:1 NIV
Now faith is confidence in what we hope for and assurance about what we do not see.

Daily Prayer

Lord, I claim these blessings over each of our journeys. I thank You for hope and new beginnings. It's often through loss that something new is birthed. Sometimes it's hard to stay focused on what is being birthed in me when all I want is what was lost. Shift my eyes to focus and see through faith. Amen.

Prayer Journal Questions

Personal Reflections...
1. What experience recently has reminded you of joy?
2. What does it mean for you to know God and be known by God?

3. What are you claiming today that is new?

4. What faith steps is God asking you to take?

DAY 20

⸙

A Rewritten Narrative

*"Blessed is the man who remains steadfast under trials.
For when he has stood the test, he will receive the crown
of life which God has promised to those who love him."*

- James 1:2

My prayer of reflection:

This morning, Lord, as I reflect over my life, I realize that my story started with hardship and adversity. I used to see this as a liability to my family and something that would impede our progress. But I have come to understand that the trials and hardships I have faced in life is my story. My story speaks of Your deliverance, it speaks of rebirth, and it speaks of reconciliation. I have come to understand that the hardships I faced were leveraged by You for good. God, you did not waste my pain, not one drop of it. You used it to propel my growth.

As a young boy I grew up in a very difficult situation. God, you know for most of my life I was angry at my parents. With Your inner work, I began to look at them with grace and mercy. I grew up in a very confusing family situation. I don't blame my parents today. I know that the mistakes that they made were due not just to sin, but to brokenness and pain in their own lives. Although my parents knew about You at the time of my upbringing, they did not understand *the meaning of freedom in Christ, salvation in Jesus, or deliverance. Sin and brokenness took hold of my parents' hearts.*

Somehow my current pain is helping me look back in order for me to move forward. The Holy Spirit is bringing healing to buried and forgotten wounds. Lord, I am surprised at the level of my inner awareness. I am finding that You are allowing this journey to till the hard soil of my heart, causing me to surrender to You what is unearthed.

I see now that my current situation, other past wounds and trauma, and my early home life, is a perfect example of You working all things together for my good. I don't make excuses for my parents' past behavior. As I look back, I believe that they did the best with what they understood and knew. Thankfully, their knowledge and awareness changed. Their destiny changed, as well as my own, when we encountered You, Jesus.

Emotional and Spiritual Self-Contemplation

As I reread this prayer this morning, I realize that all of my entire life experiences have brought me to this point. Somehow, I am the culmination of all of my experiences, of those that I perceive as good and those that have been quite challenging. I am comforted to be reminded that I am not defined by all of these experiences. Truth be told, as I reflect back, it's so much easier for me to remember more of the difficult moments in my life than the good ones. What's interesting is that this is how our human brain functions.

Somehow, we can recall the painful moments in much more detail and clarity than the life giving ones. It must be due to some sort of survival mechanism or survival skill to keep us safe. When you were a child, the first time you ever got burned by sticking your hand in the fire, you learned quickly to never do that again. Somehow, we remember that one time we got burned compared to the thousands of times we used fire to cook without getting burned. However, there's also an ugly side to our brain's safety mechanism. For some, painful memories become trauma and traumatic thoughts can cause anxiety, depression, and other emotional pains. Many of us allow our negative life experiences to become us, to define us, to redirect our destinies away from God's purpose for our lives. I hold on to 2 Corinthians 5:17, I am a new creation.

I am thankful that I am a new creation in Christ. My identity is not the culmination of my life experiences, but rather it is in who God says I am. God has carved out a destiny for my life and yours today. Your past life experiences are valuable, and greatly shape you. However, they don't define your future. Nor should you allow your past pain and present pain to steal from you. Faith tells me that God will use your experiences to build and shape you, not to tear you down. The negative things can and will be turned around for good— believe it in faith. Not only will you get through this, but it's from your pain that you will grow. God will leverage it for good in your life. That is the truth that I stand on today. It is the only truth that we all have to stand on.

Scriptures
1 Peter 1:23 ESV
Since you have been born again, not of perishable seed but of imperishable, through the living and abiding word of God;

Isaiah 54:17 NKJV
No weapon formed against you shall prosper,
And every tongue *which* rises against you in judgment
You shall condemn.
This *is* the heritage of the servants of the Lord,
And their righteousness *is* from Me,"
Says the Lord.

Romans 8:28 NIV
And we know that in all things God works for the good of those who love him, who have been called according to his purpose.

Daily Prayer

Lord, I claim these blessings over my life. I am comforted by Your unending commitment to me and your healing power. I place my future in Your hands. Thank you for never wasting my pain. Amen.

Prayer Journal Questions

Personal Reflections...
1. What do you see as you reflect over your life?
2. How have your past experiences and upbringing either equipped you or placed you at a disadvantage for dealing with this current journey of pain?

3. How can you begin to trust God today rather than holding onto your pain?

4. Have you invited the Holy Spirit to start healing other wounds from your past?

5. Being a new creation starts with a life-changing encounter with Christ. Choosing today for Jesus to be the Lord and Savior of your life starts that journey. How does being a new creation in Christ help you on this journey?

DAY 21

———— ⚜ ————

Hope Rising

"What gives me the most hope everyday is God's grace; knowing that his grace is going to give me the strength for whatever I face, knowing that nothing is a surprise to God."

- Rick Warren

Prayer to trade beauty for my ashes:

What an amazing feeling! This morning I woke up feeling hopeful, like really hopeful! The first thing I saw immediately after waking up through my bedroom window was Your glorious sunrise. My mornings have been rough but this morning was different. I find hope in You, the One who makes all things new. I am eager for Sunday service today. I look forward to connecting with other believers and letting go in worship. I feel as if there is a wall this morning holding back feelings of despair and anger. I feel a need to love; I feel a need to give, and a feeling to serve. Lord, as I think of my family and joining in on the worship I am humbled and in awe of how someone could be in such pain and still do what You called us to do. I am inspired. My family is my gift, my inheritance, my reward, my blessing that is not tarnished, that is not destroyed, that is not ruined, but rather made new. Now, I see things new. God, You have inspired me. God, You deliver. God, You redeem. God, You justify. God, You save. God,

You make all things new. God, You rescue. The feelings of hope and new beginnings are so sweet I can taste it.

We asked You for a reset this new year. What You renew You're faithful to complete. But it has hurt us greatly and deeply. I trust that the pain is part of the process of healing, purification, growth, and development for Your purpose.

I trust Your works, oh God.

Emotional and Spiritual Self-Contemplation

Today I experienced a demonstration of God's faithfulness. Though life recently has been physically stable it has been emotionally chaotic. God provided huge wins today that were much needed. They were demonstrations of His provision, His call, His love, and His faithfulness. These wins give me a glimpse of the hope that I experience now and the greater hope to come. I am excited for new beginnings!

When I think of new beginning's I think of Jesus calling His first followers to Himself. I think of that moment when He approached Peter and Andrew along the Sea of Galilee.[22] I think of the new purpose and commission He gave them. Immediately, they dropped everything and followed Him. I recognize now that this journey is a point of change in my life where Jesus has called, or maybe my ears are now more receptive to his calling me like never before. Jesus is calling you, too. For some, it's about starting that relationship with Jesus that will bring life and the start of healing;[23] for others, it's about coming to know your Savior first hand rather than in some Bible story of His deliverance of others. It's in our pain where we experience the miracle. Without the presence of a need or a need for rescue there are no miracles.

Scriptures

2 Corinthians 5:17 ESV

Therefore, if anyone is in Christ, he is a new creation. The old has passed away; behold, the new has come.

Isaiah 42:18-19 ESV

"Remember not the former things, nor consider the things of old. Behold, I am doing a new thing; now it springs forth, do you not perceive it? I will make a way in the wilderness and rivers in the desert.

Isaiah 40:31 ESV

But they who wait for the Lord shall renew their strength; they shall mount up with wings like eagles; they shall run and not be weary; they shall walk and not faint.

Daily Prayer

Dear Lord, I thank You for Your word and how we are reminded that we are a new creation in Christ Jesus. We may not always feel like it, but we are. Thank You for reminding us who we are in Christ. What we are, life circumstances cannot steal. Amen.

Prayer Journal Questions

Personal Reflections...
1. Have you had similar unexpected experiences of hopefulness?
2. What are you asking God to renew?

3. What new beginnings are you eagerly awaiting?

4. Share with God your frustrations with the waiting process.

DAY OF REST

As we prepare to enjoy a break from all that has been going on let's acknowledge that you need it. You need a break from the feelings, trying to figure things out, and the worry of the unknown.

Sometimes, this journey can feel like everything positive has been swallowed up. Throughout my career as a mental health professional or even as a pastor, I come across so many people that feel like all their joy and hope has been swallowed up by life, losses, or just by all the stress. It is so difficult for us in our society which is always on the go to stop and just enjoy life the way it was meant to be enjoyed. Ask God for courage to take another much-needed break. Things have felt very difficult lately and often when I am struggling with trying to stay positive, I stand on this promise:

Rejoice always, pray without ceasing, give thanks in all circumstances; for this is the will of God in Christ Jesus for you.[24]

Sometimes it is difficult to give thanks in every circumstance, but often it's just the right antidote to a negative filter and a chronically negative perspective. Such a perspective has the power to hurt us so deeply.

Take the day and practice gratitude. This is a great exercise because it reminds us that although we are going through a difficult season in life and experiencing loss, you still have many good things to accomplish and be grateful for. You have many good people, family, friends, and maybe even your favorite pet to help you feel loved, valued, and appreciated. The loss you are experiencing has not stolen everything. Don't forget to celebrate what you have.

You can also plan something positive. This has helped me so much in my journey. Pick something positive you have never done before or at least not in a while. Try a new hobby or do that thing you have wanted to do but kept putting off because you never had the time. Make the time and give it to God in faith. God created you, the apple of His eye because He values you. Use this day of rest to your advantage.

DAY 22

What if...

"Trusting in something other than God is another way you Edge God Out.
When you trust in something other than the character and unconditional
love of God as your source of security and self-worth. Instead,
you must place your trust in that which is sure and eternal: God's
care for you and the wisdom He provides about living in
harmony with the rest of His creation."

- Ken Blanchard

Prayer to trust Him in the journey:

I can't help but think about what life was like before pain. Before loss. I find myself fantasizing about my past work and family life. Remembering how it felt and how wonderful it was. Will it ever be that way again? Can I reclaim what was lost or stolen? Maybe I'm bargaining, bargaining with the past and the present. Could I have altered circumstances? What if? Is it worth even asking these questions? I find it difficult to help myself not ask these questions. Most of the time I don't even realize that I am doing it until I have already invested a great deal of time into this thought process.

Lord, if I can't have what was lost, how can things be okay again? How will I feel the comfort I once felt? Your word tells me that You renew all things. I have to put my faith in that somehow, even with the difficulty and pain of this situation, it will somehow be alright again. I may not understand how, but I need to trust that You can and You will. I have no other hope but in You.

You are a good God. You created me, You love me, and You have saved me. Evil does not come from You. Your desire is to restore me and my household. I trust that You will give us what we need for full and complete restoration. I trust that You will not only make all things new, but You will also restore what has been stolen.

Emotional and Spiritual Self-Contemplation

At this point in my journey, I remember often thinking or wondering how would things ever be okay again? I was confused and struggling with my faith yes, even as a Pastor! I didn't know how things would turn out or where they would go. I had no choice but to trust. I am thankful that I understood being emotionally hard or angry at God would have only alienated myself emotionally from the only One who could bring me hope and healing. He has always been my "way maker" and "my miracle worker." He is the same yesterday, today and tomorrow. Thankfully He never changes!

Imagine the wonder that it must have been for the disciples to do life with Jesus; to learn directly from Him; to love Him and to be loved by Him. Imagine, also, the confusion there must have been when Jesus died on the cross and was placed in the tomb. I believe they struggled and asked many of the same questions I've asked in the above prayer. These men gave up their lives to follow Jesus, the Son of God. Then He died and they felt abandoned.

It wasn't very long before their faith was renewed. Somehow what they longed for was no longer the thing they wanted and they realized that their pain was the cost of the victory they came to experience firsthand—Jesus rose from the dead.[25]

Although things have changed, our suffering is not in vain or wasted. Jesus sympathizes with our pain and it is through His pain that we are healed.[26] We don't suffer alone but rather we suffer in Christ who has the power to heal.

I encourage anyone who is journeying with this book to choose Jesus. Say yes to Jesus today as the Lord and Savior of your life. Submit and surrender yourself to Him and all His promises are yours. I can't imagine suffering alone. Suffering with God gives you the hope of a future and a new beginning. He is the God of new beginnings.

Scriptures

Psalm 71:20 ESV
You who have made me see many troubles and calamities will revive me again; from the depths of the earth you will bring me up again.

Jeremiah 17:14 ESV
Heal me, O Lord, and I shall be healed; save me, and I shall be saved, for you are my praise.

Jeremiah 33:6 ESV
Behold, I will bring to it health and healing, and I will heal them and reveal to them abundance of prosperity and security.

Daily Prayer

Lord, I thank You for the reminder of Your promises. I can plant and celebrate in even greater promises through the new covenant and claim them for my life. There's no one and nothing else I can put trust in that has the power to heal but You, God. I trust that You will renew my heart and mind. I trust that You will make all things new. In Jesus Christ's name I claim Your promises over my life. I trust your works, O God. Amen.

Prayer Journal Questions

Personal Reflections...
1. What was life like before your journey began?
2. What do you imagine a new beginning will look like?

3. How are you putting your hope in Jesus today?

4. How is suffering different for those that suffer with God versus those that suffer without God?

DAY 23

❦

The Solid Rock

"The spiritual law of gravity ensures that the chaos of the human soul will settle if it sits still long enough."

- Ruth Haley Barton

Prayer to fix my focus:

Every day is tough with little reprieve, but this morning is particularly tough. My thoughts are plagued with pain. I feel as if I am being bombarded with thought after thought of grief. I fight and I keep on fighting. I fight for control over my mind and heart, I fight for peace, I fight for hope. But I am tired. Part of me feels as if I do not want to fight anymore. On the other hand, I know that if I stop fighting I will be overcome. I am so tired. Scripture calls me an overcomer. Your word tells me that I can do all things through Christ who strengthens me. I need a miracle. You sustained me in times of weakness. I cannot believe that my heart and mind have survived the pain this long. I suppose, as I step back and look at these last few months of grief, it has been a miracle that we have emotionally survived it. I just feel like giving up sometimes, I am not sure how much fight is left in me. I need a miracle. When it hits me like this I just cannot get comfortable. No matter what I do, no matter where I am, there is no comfort. The only comfort that I can find is hope in what You will do.

As I pray, no matter how I feel, I am reminded that truth is not a feeling. I am reminded that my feelings deceive. I choose to trust You and Your word over my feelings. I won't give up. I can't give up because You have not given up on me. As long as I feel and know that You are fighting on my behalf, I will fight too. I will fight to believe, I will fight to hope, and I will have faith in You. Without You, everything is just utterly meaningless.

I now feel a sense of calm coming over me. I thank You for the gifts of comfort that You bring between the deep dark valleys and pits we walk. I know it is not I who walks alone but You walk with me. You walk beside me because You're my friend. You're my Comforter, You are my strong fortress, You're my salvation, You are my God, my All in All, the great "I AM."

I may not be able to stop or control my feelings and my thoughts worry and defeat at times, but it is You that brings me stability and hope for tomorrow. For months now I find myself often asking, "Why"? Why the pain? Why the loss? Just why? But I don't know, I cannot know. Maybe I realize now that I don't need to know. All I need to do is trust. I trust in the God who surpasses all understanding. Your thoughts are higher, Your knowledge is wiser, Your might is greater. Though my family and I walk through this darkness, we will choose to serve You. I trust You will make a way. I know that I am on the right path. You place my foot upon the solid rock. Thank You.

Emotional and Spiritual Self-Contemplation

Sometimes all we can do is fight; fight to press on and fight to believe. I was thankful that I had many reminders on this journey that my feelings were just a blowing of the wind. Our feelings are valuable and important both to us and to God, but they are often not an indication of truth. There is that stabilizing truth again. That's why claiming truth with your lips is a primary means of fighting; fighting for hope, faith, and strength. We wage war with our words against lies and negativity. We wage war with prayer. What we speak matters!

We can choose to speak negativity or life. Speaking life is speaking the Word of God, His promises and His truths. We speak life; life into our situation. We speak hope despite circumstances. We speak strength. Today I speak a blessing over you. I speak a fighting spirit. I speak a courageous person. You will stand firm on the Rock. You will endure and you will be victorious. Amen.

Psalm 18 brought so much peace to me during this leg of my journey. It reminded me that despite how I felt, God was and is my Shelter, my Rock, my strong fortress, my high place, my safety, my Shield, my Provider, my Rescuer, and my Redeemer. He fights for you, He loves you. [27]

Scriptures

Psalm 103:2-8 ESV
Bless the Lord, O my soul,
    and forget not all his benefits,
who forgives all your iniquity,
    who heals all your diseases,
who redeems your life from the pit,
    who crowns you with steadfast love and mercy,
who satisfies you with good
    so that your youth is renewed like the eagle's.
The Lord works righteousness
    and justice for all who are oppressed.
He made known his ways to Moses,
    his acts to the people of Israel.
The Lord is merciful and gracious,
    slow to anger and abounding in steadfast love.

Romans 5:2-5 ESV
Through him we have also obtained access by faith into this grace in which we stand, and we rejoice in hope of the glory of God. More than that, we rejoice in our sufferings, knowing that suffering produces endurance, and endurance produces character, and character produces hope, and hope does not put us to shame, because God's love has been poured into our hearts through the Holy Spirit who has been given to us.

Deuteronomy 31:6 ESV
Be strong and courageous. Do not fear or be in dread of them, for it is the Lord your God who goes with you. He will not leave you or forsake you.

Daily Prayer

Lord, I claim courage over my life today. I claim faith. I claim strength. Grant me the strength to press forward. As you encouraged Joshua to have courage I too choose courage. I place my hope in You. Amen.

Prayer Journal Questions

Personal Reflections...
1. What do you stand on, (truth or lies), when you are feeling weak?
2. What have you identified that you have believed that is untrue?

_____

3. What reparative truths do you need to claim?

_____

4. What practical steps can you take to speak truth more regularly?

_____

DAY 24

Same Old Triggers

*"A change of pace plus a change of place equals
a change of perspective."*

- Mark Batterson

Prayer to try on new lenses:

Father, I am tired of the same triggers. I'm tired of pain and I am tired of the vacillations of emotions. I am tired of the hurt. I want a new beginning. I want a rebirth of liveliness and happiness. I want to wake up to a new day. I may not be able to get rid of memories, but I want the past to be behind me and hope to be ahead. I don't want to feel held back or as if the trauma and loss is still with me. I want to live without loss. You are a God of new beginnings. I want to be made new. The days with grief overall, have been less intense lately, but when those triggers come it is as if I am right back at day one. Make me new, O God, help me to feel as if the grief is behind me. Help me to take hold of my future and Your purposes for my life. I will not allow the pain to overcome me. I will not allow it to distract me from all that You are doing in my life and the healing that is occurring. It will not defeat me. No it will not be victorious over me. I am victorious in Christ Jesus. I accept my current lot and I will trust in You, Jesus, through the work of the Holy Spirit to continue healing in my life, to continue rebirth, and a full and complete restoration.

I realize it's not fully my problems that have to change, it's my perspective. I need my perspective to be bigger than my problems. God, You are bigger than all things. You are the God that walks ahead of me. You are the God who walks with me and You are the God who walks behind me. Through You all things are possible.

I claim today is a new day. I claim today as a birthday of renewal of my heart and my mind. I call all losses, trials, storms, grief, and pain to be behind me as I walk forward. Although I will not forget and miss what was, I look forward to what is ahead. I claim today as my new birth emotionally. Today is my birthday. The old things have gone and the new things have come. Amen.

What does Your word have for me today? How can I change my perspective?

Emotional and Spiritual Self-Contemplation

Perspective is reality or at least the one we choose to live in. Our perspectives are filters that we process life through. A positive perspective will help us to see the good in things, whereas a negative perspective, can create gloom and doom over our life with a dark cloud, and we see the negative. There is power in our perspective because like the tongue, it has the power to bring life or death to your situation.[28]

Perspective is a powerful thing. It will cause us to win battles or lose a battle before we even enter it. I am reminded of the power of perspective in the book of Numbers 13-14. This is when Moses sent out the spies to report back what they found in the land of Canaan. The report was that the men found a land flowing with milk and honey, meaning it was good. It was fertile land with water, good soil, and food. It was more than enough for Israel to call home. Yet the rest of the report was that it was inhabited by all their enemies, armies, and oh yeah, giants! Here, we clearly see the power of perspective. Besides Moses, Caleb, and Joshua, the rest of the spies and Israel were already defeated by the dread and fear in their hearts. They lost the battle before they entered it. As for the three, they had already won the battle and took possession of the land before the battle began.

Too often, we are like the rest of Israel and forget that we have access to the God of the universe. The perspectives of Moses, Caleb, and Joshua were based on faith in God's promise to take over the land and not just what they saw. It was their faith perspective that brought them victory. It is also interesting to me how the faith perspective of one person can positively impact everyone else around you. It was through their faith perspective that Israel was blessed and won the battle.

You must have a faith perspective that no matter how big your giants are, you serve a God who has already given you victory and delivered your enemies into your hands. Pray today for a positive perspective. Fight for it.

Scriptures

Psalm 18:2 ESV
The Lord is my rock and my fortress and my deliverer, my God, my rock, in whom I take refuge, my shield, and the horn of my salvation, my stronghold.

Mark 11:24 ESV
Therefore I tell you, whatever you ask in prayer, believe that you have received it, and it will be yours.

1 Corinthians 6:19-20 ESV
Or do you not know that your body is the temple of the Holy Spirit within you, whom you have from God? You are not your own, for you were bought with a price.

1 John 5:4 ESV
For everyone who has been born of God overcomes the world. And this is the victory that has overcome the world – our faith.

Lord, I pray that you would calm each of your hearts and minds today. Bring us a peace that surpasses all our understanding. Amen

Daily Prayer

Today I remember that I am an overcomer. I have called victorious, a child of God, and I am blessed. Yes I am blessed indeed because I serve the one true living God. Thank you for fighting my battles. Amen.

Prayer Journal Questions

Personal Reflections...
1. How has your perspective impacted your journey?
2. What perspective shift do you need today?

3. How could Caleb and Joshua have such a positive perspective when everything before them appeared that they were outmatched?

4. How is your faith connected or impacted by your perspective?

5. How has your perspective shaped your view of God?

DAY 25

⸎⸎

Gut Check

"You cannot control the events or circumstances of your life, but you can control your reactions."

- Dr. Caroline Leaf

Prayer for strength to face the mirror:

Lord, I find people so difficult sometimes. It is hard not to get frustrated, to lay down judgment, or to not boundary myself away from them fully. People are especially difficult now more than ever. It can't just be all me. I know that through this journey my tolerances are lower than usual and I am less accommodating while I'm hurting, but it can't be all me. I think that others' unhealthy expectations, unrealistic wants and demands are just more obvious now. I am at a state where it's hard to overlook and ignore. Truthfully, though, I am off and not myself. I used to be more gracious and kind. I liked myself then.

Now I observe someone's misbehaviors and judge harshly, maybe even sometimes rightly but never giving a moment to see the humanity in it.

Through looking into the mirror of Your word the Bible stares back at me and makes everything clear. I see myself as a human who is broken and has both emotional and spiritual hang-ups. Without healing it's out of these hang-ups that throughout my life I have suffered and caused suffering. My bad behaviors, if I'm honest, have always been a result of either emotionally unhealthy or some deep pain. In my deep pains it was as if I often went through life searching for something I couldn't find.

I'm not happy looking at others with new eyes. God, give me strength to show grace and mercy. May I make room for the humanity of every individual I encounter. They are in search of what I was, that missing piece to fill the gap.

None of this justifies bad behavior. I am responsible for every choice I make even if it's influenced by my own weakness. I ask for understanding where those choices come from so that I may surrender them to You. Help me to stand strong and not run. Holy Spirit, grant me the strength to endure and to love.

Holy Spirit, give me wisdom to know the difference between a person's value and worth and their behavior; wisdom to know what boundaries I need to set with others.

It's not always easy because everything in me wants to fix or fight that which is uncomfortable. You called me to love and to love big. Because You love me, I also choose to love. I want to show kindness to those who need kindness and mercy to those who need mercy, grace to those who need grace, patience to those who need patience. I want to respond godly to those around me.

Emotional and Spiritual Self-Contemplation

During difficult times, especially when we are emotionally compromised, we have very little tolerance to what we would normally overlook. We are more irritable and less kind. Sometimes we don't even want to be bothered by others and have no way to hear or carry their problems; so we often isolate and distance ourselves. It's okay to feel this way. However, we need not sin or rationalize and justify our bad behavior because we are hurting. Our hurting does not justify us hurting others.

Let's be honest with how we feel, own our feelings, and set healthy boundaries. It's better to tell someone we are off and not feeling like ourselves than to act poorly as a means of communicating "get away" to them. Let's find a nicer way, use our emotional language and tell them in a healthy way. It's hard. I get it because I've been there and made many, many mistakes.

I think the key here is:

1. Being aware of what's happening inside of us
2. Identifying healthy boundaries
3. Communicating in a healthy emotional language: Starts with an awareness of one's own feelings and emotions and then conveying them to others in an emotionally respectful way that is clear and balances healthy values for self and others. It is honest, clear, and captures our true experiences, feelings, and emotions.

What I found that worked best for me was a fixed template: "I'm sorry but I can't _____. I am not at my best so my (boundary, patience, tolerance) is _____."

I am reminded when Jesus was grieving the loss of John the Baptist, His cousin. Jesus withdrew by boat to a solitary place to be alone, maybe to pray, to cry, or to feel His sorrow. Though Jesus was hurting He still had compassion on the crowd of 5,000. He didn't respond with unhealthy emotion, rather he had compassion and one of the greatest miracles occurred.[29] Sometimes it is in our pain that we are closest to God and in our pain is where some of the greatest miracles will occur.

Scriptures

1 Thessalonians 5:15 ESV
See that no one repays anyone evil for evil, but always seek to do good to one another and to everyone.

Mark 11:25 ESV
"And whenever you stand praying, forgive, if you have anything against anyone, so that your Father also who is in heaven may forgive you your trespasses."

Matthew 9:36 ESV
When he saw the crowds, he had compassion for them, because they were harassed and helpless, like sheep without a shepherd.

Daily Prayer

Lord, may you bless me with a calm heart today. May you show me compassion in my hurt and pain. Grant me the ability and desire to offer grace as You have shown me. Amen.

Prayer Journal Questions

Personal Reflections...
1. How has this journey impacted your behaviors toward others?
2. How has coping with others been difficult?

3. What triggers have you become aware of?

4. How can you take ownership over your triggers?

5. What do you hear God impressing upon you regarding your triggers?

DAY 26

———— ⚜ ————

Be Still, He Has You

"Be still, and know that I am God."

— Psalm 46:10

Prayer of peace for a restless heart:

Last night sleep was far from ideal. This morning I woke up feeling something uncomfortable but not sure what. I feel lots of things roaming around in my head at once. I don't feel content. I feel restless emotionally. As I think and pray further about this I realize that I just feel sad and uneasy. The pain continues. I find myself bargaining again, with circumstances, with life, with You. I wonder, "What if things would be different? What would things be like? What if certain things never happened? Please, oh, please!" But even with all my bargaining I find myself here. I really wish so deeply that things could be different. I seem to be pointing the finger at myself lately. I find myself asking things I thought I had the answers to, such as, "Why? Why do bad things happen?" To this question I know a well-scripted answer in my mind but it leaves my heart in want. My heart is not satisfied with it. My heart doesn't reason, my heart sometimes wants what does not make sense. How can You bring peace to my restless heart? What does Your word have for me?

Lord, I take refuge in Your word. I gain stability of heart from it. It calms me. It soothes me. You are a God of peace, understanding, and order. May my heart find peace and my mind stability in You. You are a good and loving God. You intend all things in my life for good. I trust You, Lord, and I will continue to abide in Your word

154

and find peace in Your hope. Heal my heart; release my restlessness as I look forward to what is being made new. To God be the glory forever. In Jesus' name, amen.

Emotional and Spiritual Self-Contemplation

It is a surreal feeling, the suffering of this magnitude. It's often a real struggle to be satisfied with the answers to questions that you had before the pain.

Why do bad things happen to good people?
Why is it that gratuitous evil exists?
Why was this allowed in our lives?
Why is my family left to suffer?

All these answers I have had and thought I was comfortable with them. I have spent years researching, reading, and wrestling. I have come up with what I have accepted as truth. I understand Scripture the best I can and the light it sheds on these questions.

Yet after personal losses of many types, the answers just don't feel right anymore. I still hold the truth, but I'm just unsatisfied with it emotionally at times. Truth and emotional satisfaction are not always correlated. I wanted more protection, I wanted more peace, and I wanted more comfort. But to have these at times seem outside the norm of human experience. I am not the only one who asks such questions.

The Psalmist David often questioned in Psalm 10, why the good suffer, but wicked seem blessed. King Solomon also asked this question in Ecclesiastes. Not to mention, Job, Isaiah, Jeremiah, and other great men of the Bible raised similar questions. I believe it's partly because we are trying to make sense of what is happening in our lives and often we are pleading for it to be removed. It may be the bargaining stage of grief. When we are hurt, it just doesn't make sense at all. It can't. Even our best answers to such questions will never address the magnitude of what we are emotionally feeling. No answer will take away the pain. In my journey, I have discovered the need to, "Just roll with it." I had to accept my pain and the journey. I couldn't change it. Only God could, and I had to trust in

His goodness despite my experience. In Him, I found peace. I took hold of an important promise that God never leaves me and He will never forsake me. He was with me and is with you today. He promises to work out all the hurt and pain for good.

You see, bad things will be experienced by all of us in this life—those in Christ and those without. However, for the believer suffering is not in vain or is wasted. God doesn't waste your pain. The promise for the believer is that God will bring *purpose* to your pain. He will leverage it for good. He will use it to build you, and to restore you. He will work it out for good. For those who chose to live without God, they are without a promise. Pain is just pain, loss is just loss. What hope is there?

I feel blessed and fortunate that I have God in my life. I have surrendered my heart, my will, and my wants to Jesus. I have His promises in return.

Scriptures

Isaiah 54:17 ESV
"No weapon that is fashioned against you shall succeed, and you shall confute every tongue that rises against you in judgment. This is the heritage of the servants of the Lord and their vindication from me, declares the Lord."

2 Timothy 2:7 ESV
Think over what I say, for the Lord will give you understanding in everything.

1 Corinthians 14:33 ESV
For God is not a God of confusion but of peace. As in all the churches of the saints,

Jeremiah 17:9 ESV
The heart is deceitful above all things, and desperately sick; who can understand it?

Psalm 119:144 ESV
Your testimonies are righteous forever; give me understanding that I may live.

Daily Prayer

I thank you Lord that you bring clarity with your Word of truth. I am grateful that when I feel confused emotionally or spiritually I can pick up the Bible and renew and re-center my heart and mind. Amen.

Prayer Journal Questions

Personal Reflections...
1. Are you finding hope in the promises?
2. What questions have you asked regarding the "why"?

3. Who do you find yourself running to for peace?

4. When you find yourself struggling with confusing emotions what positive behaviors do you engage in?

5. How are you allowing God to bring you peace?

DAY 27

⸎

A God-sized Resume

"Be still, and know that I am God."

- Psalm 46:10

Praying for a mustard seed:

Emotionally, today was an incredibly difficult day. I have struggled, I have fought, and it has left me exhausted. I have never felt so alone, so abandoned, and so desperate. Though my feelings are valid, I know my feelings are not true. I know what I feel is a lie. Yet, I feel it. Again, I know Your word tells me that You will never leave me nor forsake me. I am in agreement with this and claim it over my life. It is such an odd feeling to believe something and at the same time not feel it. I am convinced of Your truth and I reject the lie that I feel. Feeling alone is scary. I could not imagine a reality where these feelings were true. I could not imagine being so hopeless and desperate. I am so thankful for Your word and how it stabilizes my heart and mind. I am grateful that when my feelings tell me something that I am not in agreement with, I could read Your word and stand on it in faith.

Faith is a lifeline. Faith allows me to hope for healing, for things to be made right. Faith gives me something to look forward to. Without it there is no light at the end of a long journey. Without it there is no hope. The absence of faith leaves nothing and no one to hope in. Thank you, God, for faith.

When I feel alone it is helpful to remember Your resume. I must remind myself of the times that I felt You close. I remind myself of all that You've conquered in my *life and those around me. I remind myself of Your word and its life-giving truth. When I feel alone and lost, I return back to the last thing I remember that You spoke to me. I'm going to stay faithful to the last thing I heard you say. I search Scriptures for Your direction. I ask and cry out, "Father, help me." What does Your word have for me today? Please encourage me that I am not alone.*

Emotional and Spiritual Self-Contemplation

I really struggle to understand how others without faith make it through such pain. I can't imagine suffering without a hope. I can't imagine suffering without purpose. I can't imagine suffering without the guarantee that all things will work for my good. It terrifies me to think suffering is wasted or in vain. How does anyone navigate through such a dark night of the soul alone?

I am so thankful for faith. Faith is the gift of hope. It is a gift that not only seals my salvation, but it is also the hope of things to come. Without faith there is no hope, both in this life and the life to come. When you are suffering, if not for God, where else would you go? Who would you run to? What other source can bring comfort to the depths of your pain?

Some may say, "I will run to friends or my support systems." This is wise, you should do such things. Others are so valuable when you are in pain. But they are only gifts from God. They are compliments to His love and not the source of what you need. They are also human and imperfect. They will fail your expectations and not know how to fully mend your heart. But there is a God who can do all things, who *is* all things. There is a God who cares for you deeply. When you suffer you don't do it alone, but rather you suffer in Christ. You suffer in faith and that breathes hope.

I imagine Lazarus' sisters, Mary and Martha needed hope when their brother passed away.[30] Lazarus was Jesus' friend. Jesus loved Lazarus and his sisters deeply. After Lazarus had passed away Jesus showed up four days later. Martha showed tremendous faith in Jesus and said, "Lord, if you had been here, my brother would not have died. But I know that even now God will give You whatever You ask."[31]

Jesus said to her, "Your brother will rise again." Martha answered, "I know he will rise again in the resurrection at the last day." Jesus said to her, "I am the resurrection and the life. The one who believes in me will live, even though they die; and whoever lives by believing in me will never die. Do you believe this?" "Yes, Lord," she replied, "I believe that You are the Messiah, the Son of God, who is to come into the world."

You see, Martha didn't suffer alone. Not only did Jesus weep for them, He joined them in their pain. When you suffer with faith you are never alone. She believed Jesus was capable of anything because God the Father would give Him whatever He would ask for. Her faith brought her to a dependence on Jesus when she needed Him most. In His faithfulness He makes all things new. Jesus called out Lazarus from the tomb and he walked out with linen wrapped around his face and hands.[32] Martha's pain wasn't wasted and neither is yours.

Scriptures

John 16:33 ESV
I have said these things to you, that in me you may have peace. In the world you will have tribulation. But take heart; I have overcome the world.

Revelation 3:8 ESV
I know your works. Behold, I have set before you an open door, which no one is able to shut. I know that you have but little power, and yet you have kept my word and have not denied my name.

Psalm 9:13-14 ESV
Be gracious to me, oh Lord! See my affliction from those who hate me, O you lift me up from the gates of death, that I may recount all your praises, that in the gates of the daughter of Zion I may rejoice in your salvation.
Proverbs 30:5 ESV
Every word of God proves true, he is a shield to those who take refuge in him.

Daily Prayer

Lord, I hold Your word close to my heart. It is comforting to hear that I am not alone. I pray that the truth I know will overtake my heart with life. Your words are true. I pray that I will feel You close. I claim Your truths. I stand firm on Your promises. I take protection from Your refuge. Glory forever. In Jesus' name, Amen.

Prayer Journal Questions

Personal Reflections...
1. How has your faith carried you through so far?
2. What gets in the way of you believing like Martha?

3. Take some time to air out your frustrations with God concerning your feelings and circumstances. How did it feel/How do you feel?

4. What promises of God are you struggling with?

5. At this point in your journey, what is it like in the gap between the beginning of your pain and the healing you hope for?

DAY OF REST

Sometimes this journey can feel so lonely and isolating. Even when we feel close to God, we believe that everyone else has no clue what we're feeling or experiencing. We want to connect, but we don't want the awkwardness of questions or statements people make in an attempt to encourage us, which tend to be total fails. Nor do we feel like being interrogated by well intending people who care.

I want to encourage you not to allow these discomforts to cause you to further isolate yourself. Isolation is often one of the most difficult parts of a grief journey, but it doesn't have to be. God has appointed the church to meet our needs in times of trouble. He appointed the church to be your encouragement and your support when you have a need. Give them an invitation to do their job. These two Scriptures brought me so much hope in combating isolation.

Philippians 4:6-7 (ESV)
Do not be anxious about anything, but in everything by prayer and supplication with thanksgiving let your requests be made known to God. And the peace of God, which surpasses all understanding, will guard your hearts and your minds in Christ Jesus.

Ecclesiastes 4:9-12 (ESV)

Two are better than one, because they have a good reward for their toil. For if they fall, one will lift up his fellow. But woe to him who is alone when he falls and has not another to lift him up! Again, if two lie together, they keep warm, but how can one keep warm alone? And though a man might prevail against one who is alone, two will withstand him—a threefold cord is not quickly broken.

Activity is also helpful because it raises endorphins and will help you to feel better. Go for a run, engage in an exercise routine, or just ride your bike. Physical activity is healthy for your body and is profoundly wonderful in its impact on our emotional, spiritual, and mental health. It will release tension and pain that comes with grief. Healthy time spent with a friend also has similar impacts on our well-being. Isolation hurts us deeply whereas connecting brings health and well-being. Be courageous today and in faith get out and get active. Take a risk and connect with a friend.

It may be hard, but it's important to get out and be social. Just set ground rules. An example of this might be, when hanging out with friends, let them know you don't want to talk about what's going on in your life and that you just want a normal night. Enjoy your time together!

DAY 28

⚜

Living Water

"... you anoint my head with oil: my cup overflows."

- Psalm 23:6 (ESV)

My Prayer for a fresh refill:

"My cup is full," is a statement that I've heard many times throughout my Christian life. Early in my walk this was just "Christianese." As a young believer I never knew what it meant, but as I got older, I've come to realize that people mean it in a variety of circumstances. It has been used to describe the infilling of the Holy Spirit, or to describe someone's heart being full, happy, and content. I have never personally used the statement, but it has come to mean something more significant to me during this emotional recovery period. If that dramatic event that has hurt me so deeply has emptied my cup, certainly there must be a way to refill it. Though it is not overflowing today, I thank You that it is filling. It is not down at the bottom like it was when I was feeling the grips of despair and anger.

However, I am still hurting. As I continue reading Your word, accepting the support that You provide, both through Your love and connection to me, and the love that You have provided through others, my cup is filling. Although my life and my emotions continue to feel like a whirlwind, at times, I will not let that hurtful event keep my cup at the bottom or from filling. Maybe when I'm hurting that's how I need to see it. Maybe I need to see it in a way that the *bad things that happen to us do not steal or cancel out all of the good things. I realize this is a choice I have to make. I ask You, Father, to strengthen me. I ask You to bless me, and I ask You to continue to fill my cup.*

Numbers 6 (24-26)

The LORD bless you and keep you;
the LORD make his face to shine upon you and be gracious to you;
the LORD lift up His countenance upon you and give you peace.

Lord, I receive Your blessing over my life and my family. I choose this day to serve You, to feel You, to know You, and to be comforted by You. I choose to acknowledge and see the good and allow myself to feel the hurt. The hurt will not overcome me. I will be taught by it, I will learn from it, and I will grow to be the person that You've called me to be. I accept the redemptive purpose You have for my life; and no hurt, no pain, and no devil can come against that. What You have established, no one or anything can tear down. I trust the God who is my Mighty Fortress. In the name of Jesus, amen.

Emotional and Spiritual Self-Contemplation

When I first approached journaling it just felt like venting and it felt good for the moment. However, I quickly realized that it stirred more and more emotion in me. My cup was dry and empty. Somehow it occurred to me to read the Psalms and I realized that the Psalmists approached their pain exactly how Jesus did. Somehow they blanketed their pain with praise and surrender. The Psalms were wounds and heartfelt pleas of desperation that were clothed with prayer, praise, and surrender. I realized that as they shared the depth of their agony, they blanketed their pain with the promises of God. A great example of that is Psalm 91. In approaching their laments, they would start the Psalm with acknowledging the greatness of God, who God is, and their desperation for Him. Then they would share their laments, followed by the promises of God.

This is the praise blanket that was created for their pain. No, I don't know if any particular order is important. I guess the main point is that they invited God into their pain and then covered themselves or wrapped themselves up with praise as a coping mechanism for how they would approach their pain. And this is where journaling takes on a new life. I came to realize that I was going to go through this journey anyway, whether I liked it or not. I came to understand that praise would become the peacemaker of my pain. I think this is a promise for you today as well: **Praise is the peacemaker of your pain.**

This brought new meaning for me: the truth lessons I discovered and Isaiah 61:2-3, (NIV),

> "… Comfort all who mourn, and provide for those who grieve in Zion; to bestow on them a crown of beauty instead of ashes, the oil of joy instead of mourning, and a garment of praise instead of a spirit of despair. They will be called oaks of righteousness, a planting of the Lord for the display of His splendor."

God promised to deliver Israel from the ashes of life. The ashes don't mean the moment of loss or the shock of trauma; but rather the ashes represent the pain, grief and despair that follow tragedy, the journey of sorrow. In the ancient times, it was common practice to sit in a heap or pile of ashes and sprinkle yourself with it as a covering, to demonstrate a sign of mourning, sorrow, and despair. If this is a promise to ancient Israel, how much greater is our new covenant promises? I mean, each and every one of them! I celebrate the promise that Jesus will redeem your situation and take off the ashes of pain, grief, despair, and loss from you and me. He will clothe us with the crown of beauty, the oil of joy, and a garment of praise, instead of a spirit of sorrow. This literally means to wrap ourselves up in praise. More practically, to wrap up your pain in praise. That is exactly what Jesus and the psalmists did.

As I did this, my cup began to fill. This phrase started to take on new meaning. I was no longer empty. My hope began to rise and I came to understand that wrapping up my pain in praise meant that it changed the way I spoke of my pain, the way I responded to it, and eventually, the way I saw it. My sorrow was transformed because I was transformed first. I was transformed in my circumstances and you will be, as well.

Wrapping up your pain in praise acts as a wonderful filter. What does a filter do? A good filter takes out all the bad; and conversely a bad filter takes out all the good. Scripture says that your tongue will speak life or death. You and I both know that we have two tongues: one in our mouth and one in our head. The tongue I struggled most within my pain was the thoughts and words in my head. Wrapping up my pain in praise held both tongues accountable and it filtered out the bad. As you contemplate the following Scriptures may your cup begin to fill.

Scriptures

Romans 15:13 ESV
May the God of hope fill you with all joy and peace in believing, so that by the power of the Holy Spirit you may abound in hope.

Isaiah 40:31 ESV
But they who wait for the Lord shall renew their strength; they shall mount up with wings like eagles; they shall run and not be weary; they shall walk and not faint.

Daily Prayer

I fight to worship you today. I fight through the negative thinking, sadness, and hurt. I know where my strength comes from. In Jesus name, amen.

Prayer Journal Questions

Personal Reflections...
1. Are you yet at a place where you feel your cup filling?
2. Share openly with God your struggle with hope.

3. How has your faith been tested recently?

4. Contemplate any wins or things you may be thankful for lately.

DAY 29

❦

More Than Meets the Eye

*"Life has a way of broadsiding us with lessons
that we need to learn but would rather avoid."*

- Craig Groeschel

Prayer for counting the cost and the blessing:

Dear Lord, in each moment that I've experienced this darkness of pain I feel an outstretched arm, even physically, that has maintained me and will not permit me to fall further. It is a fascinating experience, such extremes in emotions. A few times in my life I have found myself here, in what feels like the darkest, deepest moments of my life. It is comforting, though, to know I am not alone as I walk, stumble, and fall. I enjoy and find comfort in the blessing of loved ones. And though I feel weak in my ability to spiritually and maturely lead my family through this darkness, I find solace in You. You give strength to the bruised, to the battered, and to the broken. I am not defeated. I stand firm in Your promises and in Your hope. My heart is in such agony, yet Your voice comforts my pain and thoughts. We will overcome. We will be victorious. What the devil meant to destroy, You have redeemed, justified, and sanctified. You are making it new.

I could not bear the thought that such evil would happen for no purpose or good. The word purpose has never meant so much to me. I have to know this is not purposeless. I choose to trust You and Your word. I know You intend all *things for good for those who love the Lord. I claim each of your promises over my family and my church family that You have called me to lead.*

Emotional and Spiritual Self-Contemplation

It's interesting how tragedy, grief, or losses of many types cause us to take stock. Not to mention the fact that life can stand still for a moment or come to an abrupt stop in the next moment. When everything stops it's only then that we see everything we have, and all the things we have so easily overlooked.

Life runs fast and hard. It doesn't stop for a moment. At this pace, we feel that we will never have a moment to enjoy this life God has given to us. For some of us, we work 9-to-5 jobs, come home, eat dinner, and go to sleep, only to recycle the next day and everyone thereafter. It doesn't stop for a moment. Is this how God meant for us to live?

This journey has taught me many things, but one of the most important points is that life is meant to be lived. You see, life is meant to have "stop" and "go" moments. In our society, we just go, go, go, but the moments where we take time to spend in a relationship with God, and in our relationships with friends and family, are what counts most. We are to enjoy life, to play, to have fun, to build memories, and be a blessing to others.

I have come to understand that life is a gift from God and we have many treasures in this life that are gifts from the Giver to be enjoyed. To enjoy them properly, we have to stop, be intentional and partake. Otherwise, we will miss it. We will miss the point of life: To love God and to love others. With the good moments, there are also some very deep challenging moments, just like the ones we have been discussing in this book and what you're living now. In my own journey of pain, I've come to understand that pain is a teacher. It has taught me to stop, to watch, to listen, to partake, and to enjoy. Somehow, the adversity has taught me to love more intentionally, to appreciate more willfully, and to enjoy relationships more thoughtfully. There is a purpose in pain and it is my hope that you do not miss the purpose in yours. Life is just as beautiful as it is difficult. It is meant to be lived to the fullest— not on autopilot. Thank God for purpose.

Scriptures

Ecclesiastes 5:18-20 ESV

Behold, what I have seen to be good and fitting is to eat and drink and find enjoyment in all the toil with which one toils under the sun the few days of his life that God has given him, for this is his lot. Everyone also to whom God has given wealth and possessions and power to enjoy them, and to accept his lot and rejoice in his toil—this is the gift of God. For he will not much remember the days of his life because God keeps him occupied with joy in his heart.

Isaiah 43:18-19 ESV

"Remember not the former things,
   nor consider the things of old.
Behold, I am doing a new thing;
   now it springs forth, do you not perceive it?
I will make a way in the wilderness
   and rivers in the desert.

Matthew 11:28 NIV

"Come to me, all you who are weary and burdened, and I will give you rest.

Isaiah 53:4-5 NIV

Surely he took up our pain and bore our suffering, yet we considered him punished by God, stricken by him, and afflicted. But he was pierced for our transgressions, he was crushed for our iniquities; the punishment that brought us peace was on him, and by his wounds we are healed.

Daily Prayer

Thank you Jesus for carrying and holding my pain. I am grateful for the rock I have to stand on. I take comfort in Your unwavering truth and Your presence. I celebrate Your unchanging love and commitment to me. Amen.

Prayer Journal Questions

Personal Reflections...
1. Share your experience of changes in emotions.
2. What has it been like to carry this emotional weight for so long?

3. Does hope feel firm in your grasps at this moment or does it feel as if it is fleeting?

4. Share your experience of holding your pain in a world that doesn't seem to slow down or make accommodations.

DAY 30

⟨⟩

A Detached Heart

"The bottom line is pray. If you're tired, sick, emotionally
overwhelmed—pray.
If you're on cloud nine and life seems perfect—pray. If you lack
direction—pray.
If you doubt that prayer makes any difference—pray..."
- Tony Evans

Praying to press forward–never back down and never give up:

Lord, I was in a powerful worship service yesterday. The Holy Spirit filled the room. As I looked around, people were laughing, crying, and dancing. I observed deep experiences. But in that moment I felt so alone again. I was disconnected. I felt far from You and from everyone around me. Yet I take comfort, and have freedom from shame and guilt. The temptation was to ask what was wrong with me, but I did not. I praised You anyway, with my hands lifted high despite everything inside me feeling the opposite.

I always feel like something is wrong, broken, or a sense of impending doom. It's anxiety. I am not a pessimist. You have given me hope. I do not wait for the next thing to go wrong. You have shown me life is about seasons and even what I perceive to be bad will be used as good in my life and for Your purposes. Though I know the truth I cannot shake the feeling of brokenness deep within me. I wait for healing, I have prayed for healing, I have pleaded but yet my affliction is with me.

Today, I am making peace with it as I realize this affliction keeps me humble and broken. In my brokenness, I need You and run to You. It's often said that people run to God when things are bad. I hunger and thirst to be with You and in Your presence. My affliction humbles me and keeps me before You. Thank you!

I am a child of God, created in the image of God. I am an image bearer and I will not feel shame for my brokenness. I am made adequate through Christ and empowered by the Holy Spirit. I thank You for those brief moments, however infrequent or short they might be, where I experience peace. They are wonderful gifts and I cherish them. I thank You for my blessings and for Your work in my affliction!

Emotional and Spiritual Self-Contemplation

Making peace with my pain and affliction reminds me of the Apostle Paul. I am reminded of his brokenness and the thorn he spoke of in his flesh. Paul himself, the apostle who healed so many, could not bring healing to himself. Somehow he realized that God had purpose for his pain. He prayed three times for it to be taken away. He pleaded before the Lord to take it from him, but he had to make peace with it. Praying to God, he heard from the Lord and the response was, "My grace is sufficient for you, for My power is made perfect in your weakness." (2 Corinthians 12:9). Paul made peace with his pain because he found that it had purpose in his life. It was through his weakness that God's power rested upon him.

This encourages me to make peace with my weakness, hardships, and pain. For when we are weak we are made strong in Christ. Thank God, you and I do not suffer alone or in vain. Your pain is not wasted and you are not going unnoticed by God.

Scriptures

2 Corinthians 12:7-10 NIV

Or because of these surpassingly great revelations. Therefore, in order to keep me from becoming conceited, I was given a thorn in my flesh, a messenger of Satan, to torment me. Three times I pleaded with the Lord to take it away from me. But he said to me, "My grace is sufficient for you, for my power is made perfect in weakness." Therefore I will boast all the more gladly about my weaknesses, so that Christ's power may rest on me. That is why, for Christ's sake, I delight in weaknesses, in insults, in hardships, in persecutions, in difficulties. For when I am weak, then I am strong.

Psalm 147:3 NIV

He heals the brokenhearted and binds up their wounds.

Hebrews 11:1 ESV

Now faith is the assurance of things hoped for, the conviction of things not seen.

Daily Prayer

Lord, I thank you that when I feel disconnected and alone You are there. I choose to place my hope in you and not my feelings. I know feelings are like the wind. They are inconsistent and ever changing but You endure forever. Thank you for being close to my heart even when I feel detached. In Jesus name, amen.

Prayer Journal Questions

Personal Reflections...
1. Have you experienced moments where you have felt detached and lost?
2. Share your experience of what holding your pain is like today.

3. Describe your current wrestle with acceptance.

4. What do you feel you are fighting or resisting in your journey?

DAY 31

―――― ⚶ ――――

Moment of Reprieve

"We give glory to God when we trust him to do what he has promised to do—especially when all human possibilities are exhausted. Faith glorifies God. That is why God planned for faith to be the way we are justified."

- John Piper

Prayer for endurance inspired by hope:

Lord, as I continue to work through my feelings I continue to feel frustrated and tired. However, there are many more moments now where I go on without thinking of things that have happened or all that has been so difficult. It's a nice reprieve and rest. Yet when those moments come, I mean, those painful moments I become triggered and I can't help but remember the pain and instantly feel as if all my energy, emotionally and physically, have been drained. It almost feels like the life has been sucked out of me. Maybe it is anxiety or a heightened state of vigilance. It's a feeling that causes me to feel like something is wrong or about to happen yet my brain tells me that it is nothing new. When these triggers happen, and I find myself stuck in thought, it is as if I'm staring off into an abyss. I picture things almost as if through a tunnel with no end—paralyzed in thought. Finding myself here is troubling and absolutely scary at times.

I thank You that You are my anchor, my strong fortress, my salvation, and my Rock. You are the things that I am not. Father, I ask that You would renew my soul, my mind, my heart. Your word tells me I can do all things through Christ Jesus that strengthens me. I believe this to be true. It must be You that *helps me continue to endure. It is You that I live for. It is You that I hope in. You sustain me. I wait on You because You are the strength of my heart. What does your word have for me? What life can You speak in me?*

Thank you, Lord for Your Word and its birth-giving life it brings. I take refuge in Your promises. I hide my family in Your arms. In You and You alone do we find peace.

Emotional and Spiritual Self-Contemplation

I thank God for days like this one. These moments of reprieve, no matter how brief they may be, have reminded me that life is still good. They were like little gifts from heaven. Like manna in the desert that fed my soul and filled my heart. They brought me back from feeling like an emotional zombie to feeling life and the precious gift of joy. I am encouraged by the anchoring truth that the Holy Spirit brings renewal to my soul.

In the early days of my own journey these were nearly nonexistent. Day after day just felt harder than the next. As I journey through my own grief recovery I noticed that these brief moments of reprieve became more and more frequent in time, and grew longer in their duration. I want to encourage you today to thank God for those brief moments of joy and reprieve that you may have experienced. If you are not experiencing one today, try to recall back to the most recent moment of peace you had and be sure to thank God for it. There are many more to come and they are only glimpses of the greater gift that is awaiting you.

The greatest gift that I gave to myself on this journey was surrender. It meant I didn't have to put up a front of strength or care about how others thought I was doing. It allowed me to just be real. I came to realize that in surrendering to sorrow was the willingness to be courageous enough to face my pain and emotions. Surrendering perceived control was submitting to the authority, sovereignty, and protection that is God. This opened the door for me to finally accept my feelings. My response to this realness was grace shown to myself. With this gift of grace I accepted my humanity, weaknesses, hurt, pain, and wounds.

For the first time in my life I really, truly accepted myself on a level I never imagined and I was okay! I was allowed to cry, hurt, and be real. I was human and no longer had the burden to act like everything was always okay. With this new release, all my anger and frustration melted away. I was emotionally frustrated because all the filtering and stopping of what was normal and healthy was creating a barrier for my natural and human emotions. It prohibited my own growth and stalled my healing. It restricted my use of an emotional language and healthy repair language in relationships. But no more! I have now tasted an inward and wonderful gift of God's grace that He has administered to myself.

I hope that you too, can experience this wonderful gift of grace turned inward. I encourage you today to give the permission of grace to yourself. You are human and so is your journeying through pain. Your feelings are normal. At times you are sad, frustrated, feeling abandoned, letdown, feeling failed, angry, and more, but it's all human and it's okay. This issue is not *if* we will feel these things, but rather, what we do with them; or how to react or respond to them. Feelings are okay and you are courageous when you allow yourself to feel and take ownership over them.

Scriptures

Titus 3:4-6 ESV
But when the goodness and loving kindness of God our Savior appeared, he saved us, not because of works done by us in righteousness, but according to his own mercy, by the washing of regeneration and renewal of the Holy Spirit, whom he poured out on us richly through Jesus Christ our Savior.

Colossians 1:17 ESV
And he is before all things, and in him all things hold together.

Psalm 73:26 ESV
My flesh and my heart may fail, but God is the strength of my heart and my portion forever.

Nahum 1:7 ESV
The Lord is good, a stronghold in the day of trouble; he knows those who take refuge in him.

Psalm 28:7 ESV
The Lord is my strength and my shield; in him my heart trusts, and I am helped; my heart exults, and with my song I give thanks to him.

Isaiah 26:3 ESV
You keep him in perfect peace whose mind is stayed on you, because he trusts in you.

Proverbs 29:11ESV
A fool gives full vent to his spirit, but a wise man quietly holds it back.

Proverbs 15:18 ESV
A hot-tempered man stirs up strife, but he who is slow to anger quiets contention.

Romans 12:2 ESV
Do not be conformed to this world, but be transformed by the renewal of your mind, that by testing you may discern what is the will of God, what is good and acceptable and perfect.

Ecclesiastes 3:1-8 ESV
For everything there is a season, and a time for every matter under heaven:
² a time to be born, and a time to die;
a time to plant, and a time to pluck up what is planted;
³ a time to kill, and a time to heal;
a time to break down, and a time to build up;
⁴ a time to weep, and a time to laugh;
a time to mourn, and a time to dance;
⁵ a time to cast away stones, and a time to gather stones together;

a time to embrace, and a time to refrain from embracing;
[6] a time to seek, and a time to lose;
a time to keep, and a time to cast away;
[7] a time to tear, and a time to sew;
a time to keep silence, and a time to speak;
[8] a time to love, and a time to hate;
a time for war, and a time for peace.

Daily Prayer

Lord grant me the strength to carry on and fight forward. As I become weak uphold me by your hand and remind me of your comfort, love, and acceptance, in Jesus name, amen.

Prayer Journal Questions

Personal Reflections...
1. What is God rescuing you from today? (Be specific: fears, thoughts, feelings...)
2. How do you have to renew your mind today?

3. Do you regularly use an emotional language to express yourself?

4. How do you react or respond to your emotions?

DAY 32

Picture of Hope

*"The world's peace is relative and fleeting because it is grounded
in circumstances. God's peace is absolute and eternal because it is
grounded in His grace."*

- John MacArthur

Prayer for brighter days ahead:

Lord, this morning You showed me a picture of hope. I was fortunate enough
to see the sunrise this morning over a mountain. I have driven past this
same mountain a thousand times, but this morning was different. You used it
to speak to me. It is wintertime and there is snow on the ground, the trees are
bare, and the animals are asleep. There is no movement on that mountain.
Everything is cold, like a beautiful winter picture. As the sun rose above this
still, quiet, cold, dead landscape, I felt a renewed sense of hope.

I feel hope because my emotions identified with that which I projected
upon this mountain. The sun illuminated its emptiness, its darkness, and its
pain; just as the Son (Jesus) illuminated mine. The Son reminded this barren
landscape of the life that is to come; the hope of renewal; the expectations of
birth. My heart desires these things.

Jesus, You are hope to me. You are my beacon of light. You are my salvation.
You are my source of renewal. Though I endure and the pain persists, I look
forward to the birth and all the things to be made new. Thank You for speaking

to me through Your revelation in nature. This natural beauty is only a taste of You and Your much greater beauty. As the sun reminds the mountain of the life that is to come, you remind me of the life to come. You reminded me that you make all things new, You remind me that You work all things for good for those who love the Lord. I look forward to the changing seasons of life. What promises can I find in Your word? What Hope will I discover?

Father, I trust You for renewal. I trust that You will give me a new heart, a renewed spirit, and joy. You are my blessing and my salvation. To God be the glory, amen.

Emotional and Spiritual Self-Contemplation

It's funny how God can speak to us through things or at times that are unexpected. I was thankful He got my attention this morning. My commute to work in the morning is beautiful and scenic. Midway between my home and work there is a breathtaking mountain and on this day I imagined the ground beneath the cold snow was crying out for sun. I imagined life returning back to the mountain. I envisioned the frozen river flowing again, the landscape turning green, the flowers and trees blooming, and the animals returning.

I can see this now in my own life. God is bringing light to my pain. This reminds me of my spiritual rebirth of faith. The Bible says we are made new creations in Christ Jesus to do good works which He prepared for us in advance. I am encouraged that my life is made new and I am given a purpose. I recognize Jesus' gift is not just for the life to come but for this one as well. Too many of us just focus on Jesus' gift of salvation being for the next life; but being a new creation is also for this life, as well. Not only is our soul redeemed, but our life is also redeemed and purposed. God assigned to us a new purpose at the moment of rebirth or reminds us of what we were intended for all along; a new calling, an awakening, a new beginning in a new season. Like the cold mountain covered in winter light is shining, warmth is coming, and new life will emerge.

Scriptures

Romans 1:20 ESV

For his invisible attributes, namely, his eternal power and divine nature, have been clearly perceived, ever since the creation of the world, in the things that have been made...

Jeremiah 30:17 ESV

For I will restore health to you, and your wounds I will heal, declares the Lord...

Daily Prayer

Thank you Lord for the moments of hope that are felt. I choose to stop, slow down and celebrate them. Moments of hope are a wonderful reminder of the peace, healing, and rest to come, in Jesus name, amen.

Prayer Journal Questions

Personal Reflections...
1. Have you experienced a picture of hope?
2. How has this journey changed your perspective, values, and behaviors?

3. What are you more keenly aware of?

4. Do you allow yourself to slow down enough for God to speak to you?

DAY 33

―――――― ❧ ――――――

Give Thanks

*"Acknowledging the good that you already have in
your life is the foundation for all abundance."*

- Eckhart Tolle

Prayer for giving thanks in all things:

God, I am learning to thank You for my weaknesses and challenges. It has resulted in greater dependency upon You. Looking back over the many months of pain and challenges I see so much growth. I see myself as stronger, more capable, less controlling, and more appreciative. Today, I do not take my blessings for granted nor overlook both the common and the unique ways You have blessed and gifted my life. You have given me loved ones, friends, health, the ability to work, time to enjoy life, and the list goes on and on. For too many years I was caught up in the busyness of life, never willing or able to see the importance of slowing down and partaking in the gifts.

As I look back, this has all changed in this process: I love more, I care more, and I am thankful all the more. It's not the pain that has changed me for good, but rather my running to Your name in the midst of the pain. The pain brought emotional death, despair and bitterness. I fell deeper in love with, not the gifts of life, but rather, the Giver of life and gifts.

One of the greatest miracles was to experience and watch You accomplish things I could not in my weaknesses and challenges. My success was not my own nor are they the result of my strength, talents, and capabilities. Any success *that I have had or will have, I have come to understand is the result of my surrender to You. God, You have done some huge and amazing things through this journey. Knowing where You have brought my family and me today, is a huge blessing. God, You are a great and faithful God, I submit my life to You.*

Emotional and Spiritual Self-Contemplation

This journey of grief is changing everything for me. So much is so different. I have found a deeper dependency upon God. I have grown to love and value my relationships like I never understood before. I have come to appreciate life. I no longer live on this hamster wheel that I have run for so many years. I have learned the gift of surrender and being present in the moment.

As we saw in Scripture in Ecclesiastes 3, there is a time and a season for everything. Today is a season I look back on and count my blessings. I am able to look at our pain as a family and see that we are overcoming it and it has not defeated us. Today is a day to thank God and celebrate His faithfulness despite our circumstances. I look at David's prayer in Psalm 22, as David understood our cries and pain well. He was afflicted with grief, pain, fear, and agony. We see how this profound experience of pain caused him to run to God; to take shelter in His name and call out His promises. David was not changed *by* his pain; but rather he was changed by the God who rescued him *in* his pain. It was in his pain that he was changed.

God is in the process of rescuing you today. His eyes are upon you, your pain and your experiences. He has heard your prayers and hears them now. Your God is coming to your aid and rescue.

Scriptures

Daniel 2:20-23 ESV

… "Blessed be the name of God forever and ever,
  to whom belong wisdom and might.
21 He changes times and seasons;
  he removes kings and sets up kings;

he gives wisdom to the wise
    and knowledge to those who have understanding;
[22] he reveals deep and hidden things;
    he knows what is in the darkness,
    and the light dwells with him.
[23] To you, O God of my fathers,
    I give thanks and praise,
for you have given me wisdom and might,
    and have now made known to me what we asked of you,
    for you have made known to us the king's matter."

Song of Solomon 2:11- ESV
[11] for behold, the winter is past;
    the rain is over and gone.
[12] The flowers appear on the earth,
    the time of singing[a] has come,
and the voice of the turtledove
    is heard in our land.
[13] The fig tree ripens its figs,
    and the vines are in blossom;
    they give forth fragrance.
Arise, my love, my beautiful one,
    and come away.

Daily Prayer

God, though it is hard to say at times, I even choose to thank you for our suffering and pain. I know that at times You allow such things to train us for the purposes of growth. It's our pain that causes us to seek after you. It's our suffering and challenges that produce holiness in us. It is a difficult concept to teach, but it brings us to You. In Jesus name, amen.

Prayer Journal Questions

Personal Reflections...
1. How have you discovered God in your pain?
2. Describe in detail the current season you find yourself in on this journey.

3. Share with God what you need from Him today.

DAY 34

⚜

Stay the Course

"How long should you try? Until."

- Jim Rohn

My prayer to hold on:

Lord, this morning I awoke with a sense of renewed hope. I don't have a clear picture of full healing or what it would even look like, but it feels like I can see through the clouds a little this morning. I have a sense that things are going to be okay, maybe an assurance. Although I still feel unsettled. It is like a heaviness in my chest and weight upon my back. It is almost physical, as well as emotional. It is such an odd feeling. Even though things have been stable now for some time, my feelings continue to tell me something is wrong or rather, things are not safe.

God, at times, it leaves me confused emotionally and spiritually. How is it that my mind and my emotions can be at such different places? Lately, they have felt a world apart. All I can do is trust in You. You are stable when I am not and You never change, even when I do. How I need to trust You! As I sit here and pray I envision You like a light in the darkness. I see a light at the end of a long dark journey; that light steadies my course. I may feel like I don't know where I am walking, I may trip over things, I may walk into things, but as long as I stay focused on making my way toward that light, my course stays steady.

Without Your light I would be directionless. I would be running from many things with no particular destination, no rest, no reprieve—just running.

I repeat to myself and I remind myself often to, "Stay the course." Staying focused on Your light I run toward shelter. I run toward rest. I run toward protection in a strong fortress. With Your light ahead of me I do not run from things but rather I run to something. I run toward Hope. I run toward my Provider. I run toward my Healer. I run toward You who makes all things new. I run toward Rest. I run toward Safety. I run toward my God. What does Your word for me? What light does it provide?

Emotional and Spiritual Self-Contemplation

I am reminded of the lost feeling Israel had while wandering through the desert. I could not imagine feeling lost for that amount of time. I am also reminded of Job and the great losses of his life. He lost so much in such a short period of time. He lost his children, his wealth, and his health. Yet he never lost his faith or those truths that he desperately held onto that were his anchors.

I thank God for His light of direction. Scripture shows us that faith is a precursor to blessing. Faith releases God's truth and power in our lives. Faith is necessary for salvation, for a relationship with God, and for the power you need in your life to press through.

What good would a belief in a rescuing God do for me if I were not to combine that truth with the faith? So I will apply my faith that He will do that which He is more than capable and has promised to do. I choose faith today!

"Staying the course" has brought me such directions throughout my life. It has helped me achieve both short and long-term goals. Even when circumstances seemed insurmountable or my goals seemed unachievable, staying the course inevitably kept me on a path toward achieving them. It is so easy to get lost in grief, in that pain, and in the sense of loss. It is so easy to be overcome by it, to become absorbed by it, and to lose yourself in it. Staying the course kept my eyes fixed on the light at the end of this journey; that is hope, that is faith, that is His deliverance.

Without "staying the course," many of us find ourselves filling our pain with counterfeit comforts. Whether it is a vice or some unhealthy coping mechanism, we try to protect ourselves from pain through the use of comforts, inevitably leaving us lost on our journey. The only true comfort will be found in the arms of Christ, with the hope of God and the working of the Holy Spirit in our lives. Running to anything else will just keep us running. Trying to bury our pain doesn't bring closure. It just pushes what we have to deal with down the road a little further only to be dealt with later. Buried emotions never die, but chase us. And we will find ourselves acting out of this pain throughout our lives. Only God fills us fully and completely.

Scriptures

Psalm 32:8 NIV

I will instruct you and teach you in the way you should go;
　I will counsel you with my loving eye on you.

Psalm 37:23-24 ESV

The steps of a man are established by the Lord,
　when he delights in his way;
though he fall, he shall not be cast headlong,
　for the Lord upholds his hand.

Psalm 119:105 ESV

Your word is a lamp to my feet
　and a light to my path.

Psalm 27 ESV

The Lord is my light and my salvation;
　whom shall I fear?
The Lord is the stronghold[a] of my life;
　of whom shall I be afraid?

[2] When evildoers assail me
　　to eat up my flesh,
my adversaries and foes,
　　it is they who stumble and fall.
[3] Though an army encamp against me,
　　my heart shall not fear;
though war arise against me,
　　yet[b] I will be confident.
[4] One thing have I asked of the Lord,
　　that will I seek after:
that I may dwell in the house of the Lord
　　all the days of my life,
to gaze upon the beauty of the Lord
　　and to inquire[c] in his temple.
[5] For he will hide me in his shelter
　　in the day of trouble;
he will conceal me under the cover of his tent;
　　he will lift me high upon a rock.
[6] And now my head shall be lifted up
　　above my enemies all around me,
and I will offer in his tent
　　sacrifices with shouts of joy;
I will sing and make melody to the Lord.
[7] Hear, O Lord, when I cry aloud;
　　be gracious to me and answer me!
[8] You have said, "Seek[d] my face."
My heart says to you,
　　"Your face, Lord, do I seek."[e]
[9]　　Hide not your face from me.
Turn not your servant away in anger,
　　O you who have been my help.

Cast me not off; forsake me not,
    O God of my salvation!
¹⁰ For my father and my mother have forsaken me,
    but the Lord will take me in.
¹¹ Teach me your way, O Lord,
    and lead me on a level path
    because of my enemies.
¹² Give me not up to the will of my adversaries;
    for false witnesses have risen against me,
    and they breathe out violence.
¹³ I believe that I shall look[f] upon the goodness of the Lord
    in the land of the living!
¹⁴ Wait for the Lord;
    be strong, and let your heart take courage;
    wait for the Lord!

Daily Prayer

Jesus, grant me the strength to stay the course and journey forward. You are indeed the lamp for my feet. May I not give way to counterfeit comforts or vices. My true hope and healing is in you alone. In Jesus name, amen.

Prayer Journal Questions

Personal Reflections...
1. What does it mean to you to *stay the course* today?
2. What are you accepting today that you resisted yesterday?

3. What do you fear you may be burying and not dealing with?

_____

_____

_____

_____

_____

_____

_____

_____

_____

4. Share your struggle with courage and trusting in God.

_____

_____

_____

_____

_____

_____

_____

_____

_____

_____

DAY 35

❦

Look to the Hills

"It always seems impossible until it's done."

- Nelson Mandela

Prayer for relief on the horizon:

Lord, I have seen a great blessing today. I feel like I am in the midst of my prayers being answered. Though my heart still grieves and there is still pain, it no longer has control over me, no longer plagues me, and it no longer frightens me. I feel like something has been released. I see the miracle within me and around me. The changes have been evident even upon those who have suffered this journey with me. My family and I are free!

I thank You, God, for Your faithfulness. I thank You for carrying me through the darkest days and nights of my life. You're so faithful! You are a God who does not fail. You are a God who does not abandon or leave. You have thought of me, considered me, and valued me. Who am I that the God of the universe should pay me any mind? Your word tells me I am your most precious possession.

As I look back, so much has changed. Things will never be the same as they were. They will be better. Things are made new. I have seen how pain has been a teacher. I see the growth, spiritually and emotionally, in myself and in those that have suffered through this journey, as well. We are closer to You, we know You more, we hear Your voice louder, and we have come to love You more.

My heart is overwhelmed with joy and peace. But what of the pain? It is still there. It is an ever-present reminder of past things. But I am not frightened by it *anymore. It has now become more of a reminder of God's greatness, redemption, renewal, restoration, recovery, and faithfulness. To God be the glory! What does Your word for me? What light does it provide?*

Emotional and Spiritual Self-Contemplation

At this point in the journey it was much more evident how God's promises have come to be fulfilled for us and in us. I would not have known God the way I do had it not been for the pain that was endured. I always knew God was a deliverer, but I did not know Him as my Deliverer until I needed deliverance. I came to know Him as my Rescuer when I was in need of rescuing. I came to know Him as a lover of my soul when I needed His love most. I came to know the greatness of God when I needed a miracle. I may have had prior cerebral knowledge of these things before, but it wasn't until I was in need that God became so real to me. I needed God to show up and He did!

As I look at Scripture, I can't help but to see this was a similar journey that you and I share with many of the biblical characters. I look at the difficulties faced by Abraham, Lot, Joseph, Jacob, Moses, Joshua, David, Samson, the prophets, the apostles, and even Jesus, Himself. In all of these examples, we see a God that is a rescuing, redeeming, restoring God. These men and many others have faced such great deep trials and God became great to them and in them through their pain. When a child of God suffers, we suffer with a promise unlike those outside of the family of God who suffer without a promise. Somehow our suffering is leveraged for good, for growth, and for life. Pain is a teacher that not only helps us to meet God, but also equips us for life and for what God has for us. It builds the strength, character, and integrity that is needed for where each of us is going and for who we were created to be.

Scriptures

Revelation 21:4 NIV

'He will wipe every tear from their eyes. There will be no more death'[a] or mourning or crying or pain, for the old order of things has passed away."

Psalm 23 NIV
The Lord is my shepherd, I lack nothing.
    He makes me lie down in green pastures,
he leads me beside quiet waters,
    he refreshes my soul.
He guides me along the right paths
    for his name's sake.
Even though I walk
    through the darkest valley,[a]
I will fear no evil,
    for you are with me;
your rod and your staff,
    they comfort me.
You prepare a table before me
    in the presence of my enemies.
You anoint my head with oil;
    my cup overflows.
Surely your goodness and love will follow me
    all the days of my life,
and I will dwell in the house of the Lord
    forever.

1 Peter 4:12-13 NIV
Dear friends, do not be surprised at the fiery ordeal that has come on you to test you, as though something strange were happening to you. **13** But rejoice inasmuch as you participate in the sufferings of Christ, so that you may be overjoyed when his glory is revealed.

Daily Prayer

Thank you for the blessings of life. Somehow this journey has stopped each of us long enough to identify all that we have taken for granted. Please forgive us for never stopping and never noticing. We stop now and thank you for what is going well in our lives, first the often overlooked common blessing of food, water, shelter, and more. Second, thank you for all the specific blessings including support from others, love, and relationships. In Jesus name, amen.

Prayer Journal Questions

Personal Reflections...
1. What is God rescuing you from today? (Be specific: fears, thoughts, feelings)
2. How much greater do you know God because of your journey of pain?

3. How has this journey opened you to God in ways that you weren't prior?

4. How do you see God starting to use and leverage your pain?

DAY OF REST

Sometimes in this journey we become so overwhelmed and focused with the pain, difficulties, and challenges associated with grief that we feel like we lose momentum, creativity and even motivation. But, on our day of rest let's agree to not allow that to stop us. This process though painful and difficult is growing you and making you stronger. What the enemy meant for disaster God is faithful to use for good. In His faithfulness to bring healing and rebirth into your life on this day of rest let's reconnect with who you really are.

You are gifted, talented, and unique in all the amazing ways God has created you. Many times, we feel disconnected from ourselves in this journey of pain and loss. We start to feel like we lose ourselves. Let today be a day of personal re-discovery. Two things that really helped me when I found myself at this place was to be creative and volunteer. Let me explain. Some of our greatest frustrations on the journey is often our inability to put our feelings into words. Most of the time words can never capture the depth of what we are really feeling. So, take this day of self-expression and rest and be creative. Paint something, build something, draw something. Creativity during the grief process can be a wonderful outlet and expression of feelings that goes way beyond the use of words and writing. You can also express yourself through art and music.

Volunteering my time was a wonderful asset and tool in my selfcare routine. For many people volunteering their time to others in need, or at your church, or even the local animal shelter takes our focus off of our own pains and wounds and allows us to feel good as we help others. This is a wonderfully healthy escape and will build feelings of self-acceptance, increase self-esteem, self-efficacy, and spiritual well-being.

DAY 36

⸺⸙⸺

Seeing God in Unexpected Places

"You made him a little lower than angels…"

- Psalm 8:5

Prayer for confidence in a God who has me:

Today, I was parked in a parking lot in front of a supermarket and I saw the most amazing thing: sparrows. Yes, a small, seemingly insignificant and unimpressive gray and brown bird. Even so, it ministered to my heart and soul. I first ran into the supermarket to pick up lunch. I was in a rush and stressed, rushing to my next appointment. Desperately trying to shove some energy down my throat to press forward. As I was just about to pull out of the parking lot I noticed two sparrows in the tree directly in front of me. Something stopped me and in that moment I was captivated. As I watched them jumping from branch to branch and their little heads rotated back-and-forth without end, I thought they were looking for bugs or seeds to eat. With all their feathers they looked like little puffballs with a beak.

In that moment, I appreciated the beauty and their creation, for the first time. Lord, in all my life, I never slow down enough to notice or even care about such creatures. There is just something about this journey that has caused me to see God in the most unexpected places. To hear His subtle voice in the most unexpected ways. The sparrows look so content, almost happy. God I hear you loud and clear; "you got me!"

I am so much more valuable to you than all the sparrows of the air and you take such wonderful care of them. What can I expect from you? Far more, above and beyond. If their needs are met at every moment how much more are mine? They are never in a rush to speed through life, but rather they are present in the moment, in your hands they are content. God, may I find that level of contentment and peace. As I watched them they just existed in perfect peace. Today you ministered to me through the sparrow. I am impacted and blessed for it. My heart is full as I am reminded of the importance of self-care, peace, contentment, and satisfaction. I am thankful! Life seems more marvelous and precious now. What does Your word for me? What light does it provide?

Emotional and Spiritual Self-Contemplation

Trials and pain have taught me to emotionally and spiritually slow down; to stop and appreciate; to stop and observe and take in. This pain journey has brought us new life. Prior to the journey we were so caught up in the race of life and business, often moving too quickly to savor it; to savor love, relationships, experiences, and most of all, God.

Where were we racing to?

What were we in pursuit of?

I don't know! We were just caught up in what we thought life was. What was expected. What we have seen modeled for us.

Those two little sparrows showed me and reminded me of a valuable lesson. I learned the value of embracing my limits and accepting I can't do it all. It is freeing. It is marvelous!

I encourage you to be courageous enough to slow down and free yourself by embracing your limits. Choose to love and invest in your relationships and those things that are most important. Be like the sparrow that is just present and peaceful. Be emotionally and spiritually present in your relationships. You were created to be a "human being" and not a "human doing." Don't regret another lost moment. God will meet your every need as we take confidence in His promises. Let's thank God that we can see Him and His hand through His creation.

Scriptures

Psalm 46:10-11 ESV
Be still, and know that I am God.
  I will be exalted among the nations,
  I will be exalted in the earth!"
[11] The Lord of hosts is with us;
  the God of Jacob is our fortress.

Exodus 14:14 ESV
[14] The Lord will fight for you, and you have only to be silent.

Job 12:7-9 ESV
[7] But ask the beasts, and they will teach you;
  the birds of the heavens, and they will tell you;
[8] or the bushes of the earth, and they will teach you;[a]
  and the fish of the sea will declare to you.
[9] Who among all these does not know
  that the hand of the Lord has done this?

Daily Prayer

God, I am in awe of You and Your greatness. I see Your bigness and thank You for Your acceptance of me and my family. I celebrate that You are bigger than any of our battles and losses. Thank You for being a God who can and will act on our behalf. Amen.

Prayer Journal Questions

Personal Reflections...
1. How has this journey reoriented your life?
2. In what ways has God spoken to you lately?

3. Has your experiences caused you to ask what is really important in life?

4. How have your values of family, friends, time, and work been changed?

DAY 37

———— ✦ ————

Repeat After Me

*"Our faith is not meant to get us out of a hard place or change
our painful condition. Rather, it is meant to reveal God's
faithfulness to us in the midst of our dire situation."*
- David Wilkerson

Prayer of thanks because You can:

Lord, sometimes I question whether I can carry this burden or walk this
journey. I'm tired, hard pressed, and I feel so weak. I would have never
imagined that I would have made it this far already. The fluctuations in
emotions and pains have been unimaginable at times.

"I will because You can" is a saying I have been repeating a lot to myself
lately. It is a powerful realization that brings hope and comes with a promise. I
feel such hope every time I repeat it. I have clothed myself in this truth lately by
simply repeating it and claiming it over my life and current situation. "I will
because You can!"

I am able to face these things because of You, my Lord. You are the
only thing that makes sense to me when the math doesn't add up in life.
"I will because You can" is what keeps me going when my strength falters
and I feel like I can't go on or take the weight. Thank You, Lord. You are
my all in all.

Overall, I am having better days lately. It makes a tremendous difference
when I choose to remind myself of Your promises. I am actively renewing my
mind by the truth of Your word and standing on Your truth. This pain and

hurt won't have the victory over me. I may be bruised and battered but I am not defeated. Those feelings of defeat are no longer allowed for me. Ever since I released myself from the perception of control and surrendered to the sorrow, I have felt an incredible release from the perceived bondage of control. I know You are fighting for me.

Emotional and Spiritual Self-Contemplation

As I remind myself, even now, of this anchoring truth, "I will because You can!"

I am reminded of the story recorded in 1 Chronicles 19 where one of King David's commanders, Joab, found himself in a very difficult and dangerous situation. He was surrounded by a warring army in front of him and another behind him. He was fighting a battle on multiple fronts. I, too, have found myself fighting on more than one front at the same time, and more than one giant in my life. All of us, even you today, have experienced these moments where we feel completely and utterly incapable, where we are spread so thin and feel like we are fighting more than we can bear.

But God in His favor gave this commander a wonderful gift: The gift of a friend. Joab had the support and assistance of his trusted brother, Abishai. With these two guys watching each other's backs and running to each other's aid when there was trouble, they were victorious. Theirs was a relationship built on trust and the assurance of a promise.

We, too, have a trusted friend and His name is Jesus. He watches our backs and runs to our need when we find ourselves in trouble. "I will because He can" is the anchor that you need to stand on today. "You will because He can." You will be victorious because He can. You will overcome because He can. He will heal because He can. He can and will make all things new; it's His promise. Invite Jesus into your situation and trust Him to watch your back.

Scriptures

Philippians 4:13 ESV
I can do all things through him who strengthens me.

Exodus 15:2 ESV
The Lord is my strength and my song, and he has become my salvation; this is my God, and I will praise him, my father's God, and I will exalt him.

Ephesians 6:10 ESV
Finally, be strong in the Lord and in the strength of his might.

Deuteronomy 20:4 ESV
For the Lord your God is he who goes with you to fight for you against your enemies, to give you the victory.

Daily Prayer

Thank you for empowering me with your Holy Spirit. The same power that rose Jesus from the dead is very much alive in me. I am more than a conqueror. I celebrate in advance the victory that is coming. I see it in faith. In Jesus name, amen.

Prayer Journal Questions

Personal Reflections...
1. What things seem insurmountable to you recently?
2. Are there areas in which you are in need of courage or strength?

3. What are you needing from God today?

4. What do you find in His Word that renews you?

5. What relationships has God given you that refresh your soul?

DAY 38

Trigger People...Again

*"Grace is the voice that calls us to change and
then gives us the power to pull it off."*

- Max Lucado

Prayer for grace extended and received:

Lord, why are people so insensitive? People that care the most can often come across as the most insensitive. What right does someone have to criticize another's recovery? What right does someone have to be opinionated on your healing? What right does someone have to call me or my family out on our healing when they have no clue what we even walk through and endured? The arrogance, the insensitivity, and the ignorance is both mind-boggling and so hurtful. It is disgusting and I am so mad!

Of course, I have to own my feelings. Yet these trigger-people make me feel as if we should apologize for not being at the point of healing that they think we should be at. They act frustrated that we still hurt and feel triggered from time to time. "Get better!" "Get over it!" "Move on!" "You need to change!" Are all things they say.

I can't help but to feel, maybe, they need to be more emotionally present, more mature, and a little more humble, maybe even a little more loving and caring. How insensitive and arrogant! God, what is so frustrating is that they are not even asked to carry the pain. They weren't even invited in. Just their sheer awareness of it makes them intolerant. What nerve!

They don't realize their behavior triggers in me deep feelings of being a burden, inadequacy, being a failure, being devalued and minimized. They are so opinionated because they have not experienced what we have. They lack perspective. If they had perspective or even themselves having experienced a dark night of the soul they would understand and recognize the foolishness of their comments.

I feel angry because I want to protect my family from people that act this way. But I can't. I'm not always there to intervene. Sometimes I feel helpless. I don't always have the right words to make the pain go away or to make things better. I feel frustrated and helpless. I am in need for Your comfort.

What I pray for is "Beauty for ashes." I pray that I can exchange the ashes I sit in for something beautiful. God, expand our hearts through this suffering. Help us to forgive, to let go, and to offer grace. It's in our suffering and being emotionally present in the journey that we are able to better understand all of those who suffer, as well. It causes us to grow in hope and helps us to enjoy life and relationships; to love better and more completely. I love people more today because the journey of pain has matured me. What does Your word for me? What light does it provide?

Emotional and Spiritual Self-Contemplation

I found that very well intended people say some of the dumbest things with the greatest of intentions. What they think is support is sometimes very damaging and hurtful. "Don't cry!" "You will get over it!" "Don't let it bother you!" "You need to be stronger!" This last one I hated the most. My initial thoughts are, *How dare you? You have no idea what it's been like!*

But what's really happening here? Broken people trying to address the brokenness in others. There is no excuse for bad behavior, but a better understanding should help us toward finding peace and closure. I don't expect others to have the answers I need or to provide me with that miraculous statement that changes everything. So I have to take ownership of my feelings and healing. I have to come to accept that not everyone is safe to share with and not everyone has the emotional and spiritual maturity to come alongside and sit in my pain with me. I also need to extend grace and acknowledge that most people are ill-equipped in their ability to navigate the hurt of others, let alone their own.

I am freed when I extend this grace and empowered to look for other supportive people in my life that get it. These are the people that I have invited to come alongside me and believe in the promise with me; to join me in prayer; to accept my hurt, and to pray for me. Only God has what we need. God is the only source of what would bring hope and a promise. Remember, His name is your promise and I cry it now. He is called Counselor, King of Peace, and Comforter.

I choose to forgive and not hold unrealistic expectations. That's the funny thing about expectations. We hold people to what we think or want them to be or act like. An expectation is only valid if two people agree. Most of our letdowns by others were broken, one-sided expectations that one person didn't agree to or were completely unaware of.

I also find value in and encourage you to use a healthy repair language with those in your life that have hurt you, failed you, and let you down. A healthy repair language is a relational commitment we make to always take ownership over our emotions and convey our feelings in a healthy way with the explicit goal of repairing and reestablishing a healthy relationship with those that we now find ourselves in conflict with.

Jesus was clear that in this life offenses would come and they would come often. I learned to overlook such things because it's healthy for me to do so. Bitterness, resentments, and anger, keep me stuck. In the end, we are the only ones sitting with a grieved heart and spirit. Forgiveness is healthy for me to give as it also releases negative feelings and negative thoughts. Life is wonderful and it's a waste of time for me to spend another moment on holding onto negative feelings.

God is the only one we can expect from. Expect His promises and trust are on their way. They may not be on our timetable but, by faith, we know He will provide them timely.

Scriptures

Ephesians 4:26-27 ESV
Be angry and do not sin; do not let the sun god own on your anger, and give no opportunity to the devil.

Proverbs 15:1 ESV
A soft answer turns away wrath, but a harsh word stirs up anger.

Proverbs 19:11 ESV
Good sense makes one slow to anger, and it is his glory to overlook an offense.

Psalm 103:8 ESV
The Lord is merciful and gracious, slow to anger and abounding in steadfast love.

Colossians 3:13 ESV
Bearing with one another and, if one has a complaint against another, forgiving each other; as the Lord has forgiven you, so you also must forgive.

Luke 6:27 ESV
But I say to you who hear, love your enemies, do good to those who hate you.

Daily Prayer

I thank you Jesus for grace. You have spared me from so much. May I be a person of love and grace. Give me the strength to extend to others what has been given to me. In Jesus name, amen.

Prayer Journal Questions

Personal Reflections...
1. Do you have a healthy repair language for navigating conflict?
2. When triggered, do you express your feelings in healthy ways?

3. Who do you have to use a repair language with?

4. Express your feelings regarding a moment someone has triggered you?

DAY 39

∽∾∽

Faith Over Fear

"Don't try to get out of the desert. Try to get as much out of the desert as you can."

- Levi Lusko

Prayer to lighten the load with trust:

Lord, this morning I find myself so filled with heartache. I am in such a place of great emotional discomfort. I feel the weight and the pressure on my chest and on my shoulders. The weight of heartache and pain is real, and it's heavier than I could have ever imagined. I am broken and battered and I am not sure how to stand under this pain. I feel like a prisoner to it at times. I hate what my life has become. It's just pain; it's just sadness and grief to find us where we are. I see before me what feels like a never-ending path of discomfort, hurt, and pain.

I struggle to share my feelings with others. I struggle with trusting them with the safety of my emotions. I fear the pat on the back answers, the shallow responses, and the quick solutions. I feel like I've tried everything and nothing seems to alleviate my pain. Lord, I am tired. I am weary. I am emotionally and spiritually exhausted. I need a fresh touch this morning. I am in need of my Shepherd, Jehovah Rohi.

I wonder what will be the outcome of all this? I acknowledge fear. I feel like I am the only one fighting, fighting for something no one else is fighting for.

And within myself there's not much fight left. But I know now, "I need to let go and let God." Giving it to You is a comforting thought because I know You are the God that can. I need You this morning to step in and fight my battles and uphold me. I am no longer able to stand on my own or able to fight any longer. I either give in to the despair or give in to You. I choose to give in to You today.

I trust that You will take my pain upon Yourself and fight my battle. I trust that You will fight on my behalf and uphold me when I am stricken and failing. I put my trust in Your name this morning – Jehovah Shalom, the Lord is peace. Amen! What does Your word for me? What light does it provide?

Emotional and Spiritual Self-Contemplation

I have lived many days like this and I have found that peace is not something that originates within me in this fallen state. In my humanity there is no peace. There is often discomfort, fight, inner dissonance, and emotional confusion. I guess I realize that the things many of us seek is because we do not possess them ourselves. Whether it is peace, hope, joy, fulfillment, comfort, or whatever it is, it does not reside or originate within any of us. So we search for it. We journey through life searching for others, for things, vices, and entertainment to fill those deep voids. But none of it will fill us for more than a moment.

We are in a fallen state and inadequate to fill the depths of our soul, only God can. I take great comfort in the shadow of the Almighty. I take stability on the foundation of the rock, and experience peace because He is my peace. The Bible has about 948 names or titles that are given to God. It is not that God is some of these things some of the time; it's that God is *all* of these things, all of the time. God is perfect. If I say God is my peace that means He is the origin of my peace, fully, and completely. He is the fullest and perfect measure of all peace to its greatest possible capacity.

The good news is that the names of God do not just describe who He is, but they are His promises to you. His name is your promise. We call him Yahweh; it means "I Am." God is saying; "I Am all things, fully and completely, to its greatest possible potential for you. I Am all things, I am everything you need. I Am all your joy. I Am all your hope. I Am all your peace. I am all of what you are looking for, and I Am all your comfort. I Am your all in all.

There are many other names of God that communicate such beauty, hope, and a promise to you and I today. Here are some to encourage you:

*Jehovah Jireh - the Lord will provide
*Jehovah Shalom - the Lord is peace
*Jehovah Rohi - the Lord is my Shepherd
*He is called Comforter, Mighty Counselor
*He is called Faithful

I take full hope in the promise of Your name. I pray Your name today over my life, my situation, and my feelings. I claim that the Lord is peace over my life today and experience Your peace, Your perfect peace to its greatest unimaginable potential. Amen.

Scriptures

2 Peter 3:9 ESV
The Lord is not slow to fulfill his promise as some count slowness, but is patient toward you, not wishing that any should perish, but that all should reach repentance.

2 Corinthians 1:20 ESV
For all the promises of God find their Yes in him. That is why it is through him that we utter our Amen to God for his glory.

Hebrews 10:23 ESV
Let us hold fast the confession of our hope without wavering, for he who promised is faithful.

Daily Prayer

I thank You that You are "The Great I Am." It is a reminder that You are all that I need and there is no shortcoming or inadequacy in You. You are all that I need fully and sufficiently. I am blessed to serve the Holy God. May I find comfort in Your name. Amen.

Prayer Journal Questions

Personal Reflections...
1. What is God rescuing you from today? (Be specific; fears, thoughts, feelings, and more)
2. What have you discovered about yourself through this journey?

3. Contemplate the struggle of trust and faith.

4. What name of God do you find yourself claiming today?

DAY 40

⎯⎯⎯⎯ ❦ ⎯⎯⎯⎯

Trading My Sorrow

*"I'm trading my sorrow
I'm trading my shame
I'm laying it down for the joy of the Lord..."*
- Darrell Evans

My prayer for the great exchange-time for a shift:

Lord, I feel so weepy today. I think I have turned a corner and finally surrendered myself to the sorrow. I'm allowing myself to journey down this path of sorrow and grief. I now realize that much of my recent anger, frustration, and feeling stuck, is due to not surrendering myself to sorrow. Fighting and controlling has kept me from vulnerability and acceptance of my pain, reality, and emotional weakness. Surrendering to the sorrow, I recognize is surrendering my shield, my weapons, and all my certainty to You. From a young child I have been programmed to fight and to look for a fight. I have responded with control and aggression, at times, to perceived threats and life stressors. I now realize it's because I'm scared. What I fear is not the fight, but rather weakness, vulnerability, and hurt. I have operated in a way as if my tenacity, desire to fight, and control would somehow protect me from the pain; but rather it has caused me to be stuck, and not surrender to You. This in turn, has increased the pressure and pain I feel.

Letting go of control scares me. I fear not being protected, a feeling that was reminiscent of my childhood. Maybe I have a belief that if I don't have control and fight, no one will protect me. But God, Your name is Jehovah Rohi: the

Lord is my Shepherd. The Lord is my Protector. Ironically, allowing myself to sit in the sorrow, feels like a release. The weight and the pressure of trying to hold the world together and trying to protect myself and everyone else is a burden too great to bear. I was blinded to this unhealthy lifestyle most of my life. I now lay down my sword and shield to fight and protect. Sitting in my sorrow, in the abyss of the unknown, leaves me with nothing but trust in You. I am so weak.

I have felt unprotected my whole childhood. This feeling of under-protection or lack of safety, has caused me to develop deep fears of rejection, being devalued, and of being emotionally abandoned. All I wanted as a child was to feel safe and protected. What tends to come out in my behaviors when challenges arise, especially relational, is a scared, reactive 8-year-old. Lord, in this journey through the fire I have found that You want to heal that inner little boy. Thank You for Your care and concern for me and my wounds. Amen. What does Your word have for me? What light does it provide?

Emotional and Spiritual Self-Contemplation

I found myself crying at times without even knowing why, and this coming from someone who never cries. But as I considered my feelings and emotions I realized that this journey softened my heart, though not in a weak way. I am now more capable to connect with the emotions and pains of others. I was more courageous now to allow myself to feel and to sit with what I felt. I was made stronger.

Life patterns put us at such a great disadvantage when dealing with difficult things. If my family of origin modeled and taught me how to deal with grief, maybe I would have handled this journey differently. Instead, it was something that we did not deal with at all. Part of why I struggled with hope was because no one ever modeled for me how to grieve well or in a healthy way.

As a child I was taught boys don't cry! I was taught not to show weakness, and to always be strong. I was taught to hold it together for others and to put difficult things behind you. Above all else, just push forward.

In my home we were not taught how to value our feelings, emotions or experiences. I was not taught how to suffer well, or to hope in faith.

Bottom line, Jesus may be in our hearts and minds, but the application of His truth does not always translate into our behavior. We have to allow the truth of Scripture to go from our ears, to our hearts and minds, into our hands, and then become actions. It's only through the truth of Scripture becoming an action that we experience transformation. Looking at the life of others in Scripture, their suffering teaches us how to suffer well, with faith and with hope.

As I think of suffering well, I remember the story in 1 Samuel of Samuel's mother, Hannah. Hannah was not able to bear children. If that wasn't bad enough, she was attacked and provoked by her enemy, which just happened to be her husband's other wife. This sister-wife provoked her violently until she wept and would not eat. It seems like Hannah's pain brought her into a depression. Scripture says she became deeply troubled and was in agony before God. Poor Hannah was in so much agony that the priest Eli, upon observing her thought she looked so bad he concluded she must have been drunk on wine. She responded to him and shared the depth of her pain. In a very healthy way, she ran to the Lord in the depth of her agony. She used an emotional language to express her troubles to another human being and she waited and depended on the Lord. She cried out to the Lord in faith with hope until He responded. God responded to her faith suffering and provided her with a son.

Reading 1 Samuel 2:1-11, you will see her prayer of praise, surrender, and desperation. She was victorious in faith long before her season of pain had ended.

I am thankful for the Scriptures and stories like these that help me to learn how to suffer well; to not rely on what was taught to me, but rather to learn from this new culture and family that I am in as a new creation in Christ. We are now in the family of God and faith. It operates so differently from what I first learned. Thank You, God, for teaching us a different life-giving way to suffer well; to suffer with hope, with a promise, with faith, and with a big God.

Scriptures

1 Samuel 2:1-10 ESV

And Hannah prayed and said,
"My heart exalts in the Lord;
   my horn is exalted in the Lord.
My mouth derides my enemies,
   because I rejoice in your salvation.
"There is none holy like the Lord:
   for there is none besides you;
   there is no rock like our God.
Talk no more so very proudly,
   let not arrogance come from your mouth;
for the Lord is a God of knowledge,
   and by him actions are weighed.
The bows of the mighty are broken,
   but the feeble bind on strength.
Those who were full have hired themselves out for bread,
   but those who were hungry have ceased to hunger.
The barren has borne seven,
   but she who has many children is forlorn.
The Lord kills and brings to life;
   he brings down to Sheol and raises up.
The Lord makes poor and makes rich;
   he brings low and he exalts.
He raises up the poor from the dust;
   he lifts the needy from the ash heap
to make them sit with princes

and inherit a seat of honor.
For the pillars of the earth are the Lord's,
    and on them he has set the world.
"He will guard the feet of his faithful ones,
    but the wicked shall be cut off in darkness,
    for not by might shall a man prevail.
The adversaries of the Lord shall be broken to pieces;
    against them he will thunder in heaven.
The Lord will judge the ends of the earth;
    he will give strength to his king
    and exalt the horn of his anointed."

Jeremiah 31:25 ESV
For I will satisfy the weary soul, and every languishing soul I will replenish.

Philippians 4:6-7 ESV
Do not be anxious about anything, but in everything by prayer and supplication with thanksgiving let your requests be made known to God. And the peace of God, which surpasses all understanding, will guard your hearts and your minds in Christ Jesus.

Isaiah 12:2 ESV
"Behold, God is my salvation; I will trust, and will not be afraid; for the Lord God is my strength and my song, and he has become my salvation."

Daily Prayer

Like Hannah, in my pain and recovery I lift Your name High. I remember Your faithfulness and boldly bring to You my prayers and petitions. I do so knowing Your proven commitment to me. You are my hope and salvation. In Jesus name, amen.

Prayer Journal Questions

Personal Reflections...
1. How did your family of origin teach you to deal with your pain?
2. How did your family teach you to deal with conflict and emotions?

3. Do you use an emotional language to express yourself: Your needs, wants?

4. How does the idea of letting go of control make you feel?

5. How does Hannah's story validate your own?

CLOSING THOUGHTS

Rejoice in the Lord Always...

"We can either journey well or journey poorly. Journeying well means running to the name of God and finding shelter in His arms of protection and receiving His hope."

- Armando Palazzo

You have found yourself at the end of this book weeks, months, a year, or more, after a significant loss. It is my hope that this devotional book has been a support to you in your time of pain, need, and difficulty. It has been my gift in honor to journey with you. I hope that you met God in the process in a deeper, more significant way. I hope you see Him as your strong fortress, your helper in time of need, and your savior. I encourage you as you go forward in your journey to look back over your journal. It charts where you have been and where God has brought you. It shows you God's resume of faithfulness in your life and just how far you've come. The journey for many is certainly not over after a 40-day devotion. You can always go back and jump into a specific day of devotion that relates to where you are in your journey. Grief is not a one time event, nor is this book, so use it as a future resource.

As I now look back over my journey through grief, loss, and pain I recognize tremendous growth. It is so evident to me in all areas of my life. My heart and soul have been expanded. I know Jesus, my Savior, now in a way I have never known Him before. I can comfortably say I know God and I am known by God.

There was a time in my life, where to encourage my faith I would read stories in the Bible of how God brought Israel out of danger and despair time and time again. I was only able to look at these stories in history to see that God has a resume of faithfulness and security, but this was other people's lives and other people's stories. Now, after my own journey, I only need to look back at my own story. I see how God has rescued me from certain peril, pain and despair. I have tasted the goodness of God, His rescue, and His faithfulness. I have seen Him become my strong fortress. I see His resume in my life and my faith is encouraged by His faithfulness.

This journey through the fire of pain brought such deep feelings and emotions to the surface, things I would have never faced or allowed myself to look at before. Yet now I was forced to. It made me feel so completely inadequate. I came to realize how for my whole life I have sought for control in nearly every situation. It wasn't until the wrestling of this journey and with the many triggers that I recognized I had a serious control issue. The opposite of faith is certainty, and I have spent my whole life trying to create and look for certainty in all of my life situations: certainty in raising my kids; with my finances; and with virtually all of my decisions. It is a sobering reality to realize that I cannot control or protect everything.

I also came to recognize that many of the things and comforts I chased never resided within myself and many of the comforts that I have sought in my life have been in an attempt to regain perceived control. What I really wanted only resided in God and originates with Him. I now get it! He is my "All in All!" His attributes are what I have sought after. He is my Peace, Provider, and Comforter. His name is my promise and your promise today.

Furthermore, I came to understand that throughout my life I was compensating for fear of failure, fear of the unknown, fears of abandonment, of not being protected, and insecurity. I have learned so much about myself throughout this process. Grief, pain, and loss have taught me much about life and about myself. It has helped me to rearrange and prioritize my life.

It has also helped me to learn the importance of stopping, partaking, and enjoying life and the many blessings God has given me.

I now see the unhealthy patterns and the burdens of trying to manage life with the misperception of control, of all things; being the protector of others and the burden of holding things together. I learned that I need to have faith and not the expectation of certainty. I have to be careful of the expectations that I place on others and myself. Prior to this journey I have never tasted the freedom of not being in control. I found giving up control to God is freedom. It is a blessing to feel I don't need to hold the world together. I am limited in my ability to protect myself fully, to protect my wife, my kids, and others that I care about. I recognize God's sovereignty and I've learned to trust Him in depths I could have never imagined.

It was only through this journey that I came to recognize how much I have been holding back from God. It was through losing something great that I have received something greater. It became real to me that God won't take something from my hand without placing something greater in it. I had to learn to let go.

This journey has freed me from many of those things. If I had to do it all over again I certainly would not choose, naturally, to go through the pain that we went through. However, I recognize that for some of the growth that my family and I have personally experienced, they would not have come through by any other means. We had to go through the journey in order to grow, and mature both emotionally and spiritually. We had to go through the journey to meet God in a way that we have never been open to before. In some respect, the pain has saved me or at very least was a tremendous catalyst of growth and faith in my life.

I also learned some really wonderful things about my family and myself:
I learned that we are creative.
I learned that there is a tenacity about us.
I learned that we are strong.
I learned that we come together and fight side by side.

I learned they got my back as I got theirs.

I learned that we can endure more things than I could never have imagined.

I learned that we have hearts that are loving and kind.

I learned that life is about loving God and loving others well.

I learned that I can be OK, even when everything around me is chaotic.

I learned that I am not alone.

I learned how to have compassion and extend grace toward others.

I learned to accept myself.

I learned how to lean on and trust God.

I learned that praise is the peacemaker of my pain.

You too have learned some things about yourself:

You are strong.

You are courageous.

You can take a hit greater than you could have ever imagined and you are still standing. You are a fighter.

You are a survivor.

"You will because He can."

People say trust, but I've always asked how. Faith is action, not just a belief. My suffering increased my faith! Like the many great men and women in Scripture, the way we journey through our pain is what makes the difference. We can either journey well or journey poorly. Journeying well means running to the name of God and finding shelter in His arms of protection and receiving His hope.

Some people say time will heal wounds. I don't believe that. I have seen many people in counseling and church still struggling with what began for them 30 years ago. What we all need is hope, directions, and a touch from God. Hope heals wounds. Like David, we have to run to and surrender the pain to God. Run to Him in our darkest moments and remember His promises. Only God can help us to find purpose in our pain. We may not see it now, but we have to believe that our pain is not wasted. Somehow a faithful God will leverage our pain for good. Your pain has purpose. It is a good God that can turn around the difficulties of our lives.

Healing Through Self-Care

Well, it looks like our journey together has come to an end. It has been my gift and honor for you to Journey with me in my pain and having invited me into yours. I am glad we have had the privilege of journeying together through some difficult times. In this life we will all face grief and the aftermath of any significant loss. You can grab any two people that have experienced the same loss and one inevitably will fare better than the other. I'm not sure why this is. Each of us, as human beings, have different tolerances to the depth of pain we feel and can endure. We each cope with and manage it differently. Some are more resilient than others.

Maybe it's due to upbringing. Maybe it's due to inner strength. Maybe it's personality and temperament. Maybe it's what was taught and modeled for us. Maybe it's all of these things. In any event, our journeys are similar, yet distinctly different. It is my encouragement that each of you will feel the freedom, courage, and desire for self-care. You can create an infrastructure of support for yourselves that will help you through your grief. For some, that may mean continued prayer, journaling, and wrapping up your pain in praise. For others, it may also mean continuing your journey through the addition of joining a grief recovery support group, seeking pastoral care, inviting the support of a loving and caring church, seeing a counselor, and perhaps even a psychiatrist.

There is a thing called *complicated grief.* As you now well know, grief is a normal response to any significant loss, such as: the loss of a loved one, a dear pet, a career, a bad diagnosis, or financial ruin. This type of grief or bereavement is a time of intense sorrow, but slowly these feelings ease and eventually there is acceptance and the ability to move forward. However, for some, they experience *complicated grief.* This is a type of grief that is debilitating and does not ease over time. Debilitating grief often impacts not just emotions but also how we function. Without additional help and support recovery is often very difficult, as this type of grief can be long-lasting and severe.

For those of you that are facing this kind of grief and loss you may need a higher level of care and support. Feel encouraged by this because there is help and support for our weary souls when suffering. This season will come to an end and there is a good life, a healthy life, and a fun one, after grief.

There is no shame in self-care or recovery. There is only freedom when we know how to cope in a healthy way. Whatever you do, don't isolate yourself. Don't leave yourself alone; doing so will inevitably cause you to get stuck in your journey and delay healing. By the end of this devotional we are all still hurting and struggling along our journeys. There is no quick fix for the type of challenges and losses that you have had. Only hope, prayer, faith, community in the church, and a trust in a God who hears our cry.

It is my hope that you continue to journey well. That you feed your soul and your heart. Continue to practice emotional and spiritual self-care. Continue to share your heart with your support systems, the people God has placed in your life to love and support you. Continue to read the word and have God reveal Himself to you. Pray and journal.

I hope that my pain and personal journey has validated yours and that you have found a voice for your pain. I hope that you see the value of wrapping your pain up in praise and have come to the hope that you are not journeying alone. Jesus is with you today. I continue to remind myself of what I discovered. Praise kept my head above water. Praise kept me from internalizing my wounds and not healing. Praise brought hope.

I am reminded to run to His name. It is said that God is given over 948 names or titles in the Scriptures. Each name of God is a promise that I claim over both you and I. His name is our promise. As I come to the end of this devotional, what's more apparent to me than ever is that God is close to the brokenhearted. I take comfort in knowing God is close to me today and He is close to you right now.

In closing, I send you off into your journey of restoration with this blessing recorded in the book of Numbers, Chapter 6. It was a blessing Moses would pray over Israel. I claim this promise over you and your family today.

"May the Lord bless you and keep you;
may the Lord make his face to shine upon you and be gracious to you;
may the Lord also lift up his countenance[c] upon you and give you peace. And
to that I add he who once came, Jesus - He is your hope and will
come again." Amen.

ABOUT THE AUTHOR

Armando Palazzo is the lead Pastor of Fusion Church in Fishkill NY. He also has an MA in Counseling and currently works not only as a pastor, but bi-vocationally as a licensed mental health Counselor/Therapist in New York and New Jersey. In his practice of psychotherapy, he provides individual therapy primarily to adults and works with families and groups. He specializes in the facilitation of interpersonal and social skills, communication skills, and the treatment of various disorders. He married his long-time best friend, Jo Marie, for 21 years. Together they parent four wonderful children. His oldest two attend college while their younger two children are currently attending high school.

Armando believes that it's in our pain that we need to find help, we need to find community, and most of all, we need to find God. What Armando discovered in his pain in penning his first book, *Battle to Win*, is that you don't have to know "how" God will give you the victory, you just have to know "Who!"

Armando can be reached online at:

Website:
www.battletowinbook.com

Emails:
apmedia321@google.com
Battletowinbook@google.com

Facebook:
http://facebook.com/battletowinbook
https://www.facebook.com/armandopalazzo12
Find Armando Palazzo on Instagram:
@battle_to_win_book
@armandopalazzo1

Resources

Emotionally Healthy Spirituality
by Peter and Geri Scazzero

Grieving with Hope: Finding Comfort as You Journey Through Loss
by Samuel J. IV Hodges and Keith Leonard

Through the Eyes of a Lion: Facing Impossible Pain, Finding Incredible Power
by Levi Lusko and Steven Furtick

Unshakable Hope: Building Our Lives on The Promises of God
by Max Lucado

Walking With God through Pain and Suffering
by Timothy Keller

The Grief Recovery Handbook: The Action Program for Moving Beyond Death, Divorce, or Other :osses including Health, Career, and Faith.
by John W. James and Russell freedman

Endnotes

1. Read Matthew 4:1-11; Mark 1:12-13; Luke 4:4-13
2. Mark 14:33-34
3. Read John 12:23-28
4. Read John 19:28-42
5. See Psalm 3
6. Philippians 1-4
7. Isaiah 54:17
8. Mark 14:32-26
9. Matthew 6:34
10. Acts 10:34
11. Daniel 6:1-28
12. Ephesians 4:26
13. Romans 8:28
14. Romans 8:31
15. 2 Corinthians 12:9-11
16. Matthew 11:30
17. Luke 4:1-13
18. Proverbs 6:31
19. David Wells, Losing our Virtue, p. 133
20. Read Hebrews 4:15
21. Read Romans 8:28
22. Read Matthew 4:18-22
23. Read John 3:16-18
24. 1 Thessalonians 5:16-18 (ESV)
25. Read John 19-20
26. Read Isaiah 53:4-5
27. Read Psalm 18: 2-19

28. Read Proverbs 18:21
29. Read Matthew 14:1-21
30. Read John 11
31. Read John 11:21-27
32. Read John 11-38:41-44

For Bookings & More Information
Visit: <u>www.battletowinbook.com</u>